Sensory Integration and the Child

by A. Jean Ayres, PhD
with assistance from
Jeff Robbins

Published by

WESTERN PSYCHOLOGICAL SERVICES
PUBLISHERS AND DISTRIBUTORS
12031 WILSHIRE BOULEVARD
LOS ANGELES, CALIFORNIA 90025

A DIVISION OF MANSON WESTERN CORPORATION

Sensory Integration and the Child
Library of Congress Catalog Card Number: 79-66987
International Standard Book Number: 0-87424-158-8

THIRD PRINTING.................... NOVEMBER 1980

To
Parents of Children
with Problems
and to
Children with Problems

TABLE OF CONTENTS

I. SENSORY INTEGRATION AND THE BRAIN

II. SENSORY INTEGRATIVE DYSFUNCTION

III. WHAT CAN BE DONE ABOUT THE PROBLEM

LIST OF FIGURES

PREFACE

Mothers of children with problems carry a tremendous emotional load. Few occupations carry as much, and those that do carry a different kind. Fathers of neurologically handicapped children do not escape from the burden, but they carry it differently.

Sometimes the weight of the problem seems too much to bear, and the presence or severity of the problem is denied in order to cope. Or parents recognize the severity and then they search and search for better answers to a difficult situation.

This book will not end that search, for it does not have all the answers; but it will give many parents the opportunity to understand their child better. The greater the understanding of a problem, the more effectively it is helped. This book was written to promote that understanding.

A. Jean Ayres
Torrance, California
March, 1979

I

SENSORY INTEGRATION
AND THE BRAIN

CHAPTER 1

WHAT IS SENSORY INTEGRATION?

Some problems, like measles or broken bones or poor eyesight, are obvious. Others, such as the problems underlying slow learning and poor behavior, are not obvious. Slow learning and poor behavior in children are often caused by inadequate sensory integration within the child's brain. These sensory integration problems are not obvious, yet they are widespread among children throughout the world. They cause some bright children to have trouble learning in school, and they cause poor behavior in some children who have fine parents and a good social environment.

Because sensory integrative problems are not obvious, yet cause so much trouble, they need to be explained. Very few people think about the brain, and so the words "sensory" and "integration" probably do not mean much to you. Sensory integration* occurs automatically in most people, and so we tend to take it for granted—just as we take our heartbeat and digestion for granted.

Unless the problem is severe, sensory integrative dysfunctions will often be overlooked by anyone who is not trained to see them. Since the brain is something that doctors study in medical school, you might assume that physicians know about sensory integrative disorders. However, most pediatricians, family doctors, and psychiatrists will not see a sensory integrative problem even when it exists. School principals and teachers do not always realize the nature of the problem. Those parents who spend time observing their children are more likely to see the problem, but without knowledge about the nervous system, they cannot understand just what is going on inside the child.

Since you may not be used to thinking of the brain as the director of all activity in the body and mind, this book will introduce you to a new way of looking at learning and behavior. It will help you understand some aspects of being human that most people never consider. Once you

---

*A glossary at the end of the book will help you with the meaning of some terms.

become aware of the process of sensory integration in your child, you will be able to notice a problem if it does occur. As you become more sensitive to sensory integrative functions in your child, you may be able to help him overcome those problems and lead a happier, more successful life.

Some Notes About Words

The purpose of words is communication. However, many words mean certain things only to particular people, and those words may mean something else, or even nothing, to other people. We want to define the words we use because this will help you know what we mean. If you don't know the meanings of our words, you cannot understand our ideas. So let's talk about words.

In this book we shall call the child *he* and the parent, teacher, or therapist *she*. We do this only because it makes our sentences simple and easy to read. Of course, most of the *hes* in this book could be a girl or boy; and fathers, too, can do many things to help their children develop. When we speak of "young children," we are referring to children under eight or nine years of age.

The nervous system is the interconnected network of nerve cells that is distributed throughout the body. The tightly packed nerve cells inside the skull make up the brain. The bundle of nerve cells extending up and down the backbone is called the spinal cord. The brain and spinal cord together are known as the central nervous system. The nerve cells outside the central nervous system are spread throughout the skin, muscles, joints, internal organs, and sense organs of the head.

We say "nervous system," but do not use the word *nervous* in any other terms. This is because *nervous* has come to mean a state of uneasiness. Instead, scientists use the word *neural* to indicate that something is an aspect of the nervous system. A *neural process* is something the nervous system does in an orderly progression. *Function* comes from the Latin word for *perform*, and so a *neural function* is the way the nervous system performs a job. A *neuroscientist* is someone who does laboratory research on the parts of the nervous system and their functions.

Sensations are energies that stimulate or activate nerve cells and initiate neural processes. You are able to read this book because light waves stimulate the nerve cells in your eyes and initiate sensory processes in your brain. Sound vibrations, touch on the skin, odor, muscular activity, and the pull of gravity are other energies that produce sensation.

Integration is a type of organization. To integrate is to bring together or organize various parts into a whole. When something is integral, its parts work together as a whole unit. The central nervous system, and especially the brain, is designed to organize countless bits of sensory information into a whole integral experience.

We use the word *tell* in sentences such as, "Sensations tell the brain what the body is doing," and "The brain tells the body what to do," because nerve cells do communicate with each other. Scientists would use more technical terms, but such terms are usually confusing to people who do not use them on a daily basis. Since this book is specifically for parents, we shall use as much simple, everyday English and as many analogies and metaphors as we can without being inaccurate.

The word *physical* refers to everything that is measurable in terms of mass, energy, space, and time. Gravity, distance, form, light, vibration, movement, and touch are physical; thoughts and memories are not physical, although they are produced by physical activity in the brain. The *physical environment* is the world in which things tend to fall down, heavy things are hard to move, two things cannot be in the same place at the same time, sharp things cut, things do not move unless they are pushed or pulled, and actions have very definite consequences. A *physical interaction* is a relationship that is governed by the unalterable laws of physics. A child reading a book has both a physical and a mental relationship to the book. The physical interaction involves holding the book up against the pull of gravity, holding his head upright, aiming his eyes at the lines of print, and recording in his brain that there are dark marks on a white background. His mental interaction involves translating those marks into syllables, words, and sentences, as well as thinking about the meaning of those sentences.

Sensory Integration Is . . .

Sensory integration is the organization of sensation for use. Our senses give us information about the physical conditions of our body and the environment around us. Sensations flow into the brain like streams flowing into a lake. Countless bits of sensory information enter our brain at every moment, not only from our eyes and ears, but also from every place in our bodies. We have a special sense that detects the pull of gravity and the movements of our body in relation to the earth.

Directing the Traffic

The brain must organize all of these sensations if a person is to move and learn and behave normally. The brain locates, sorts, and orders sensations—somewhat as a traffic policeman directs moving cars. When sensations flow in a well-organized or integrated manner, the brain can use those sensations to form perceptions, behaviors, and learning. When the flow of sensations is disorganized, life can be like a rush-hour traffic jam.

Nourishing the Brain

Sensory integration is the most important type of sensory processing. You know that food nourishes your body, but it must be digested to do so. You can think of sensations as "food for the brain"; they provide the energy and knowledge needed to direct the body and mind. But without well-organized sensory processes, sensations cannot be digested and nourish the brain.

Making a Whole from Parts

Sensory integration "puts it all together." Imagine peeling and eating an orange. You sense the orange through your eyes, nose, mouth, the skin on your hands and fingers, and also the muscles and joints inside your fingers, hands, arms, and mouth. How do you know that it is one single orange, rather than many different oranges? What makes your two hands and 10 fingers all work together? All the sensations from the orange and all the sensations from your fingers and hands somehow come together in one place in your brain, and this integration enables your brain to experience the orange as a whole and to use your hands and fingers together to peel the orange.

Sensations and Meaning

Sensations are streams of electrical impulses. Biochemicals are also involved in producing impulses. These impulses must be integrated to give them meaning. Integration is what turns sensation into perception. We perceive our bodies, other people, and objects because our brain has integrated the sensory impulses into meaningful forms and relationships. As we look at the orange, our brain integrates the sensations from our eyes so that we experience its color and shape. As we touch the orange, the sensations from our fingers and hands are integrated to form the knowledge that it is rough on the outside and wet inside. The integration of sensations from the nose tells us that the orange has a citrus odor.

Sensory Integration in Life

Sensory integration begins in the womb as the fetal brain senses the movements of the mother's body. An enormous amount of sensory integration must occur and develop to produce crawling and standing up, and this happens in the first year of life. Childhood play leads to a lot of sensory integration as the child organizes the sensations of his body and gravity along with sight and sound. Reading requires very complex integration of sensations from the eyes, eye and neck muscles, and the special sense organs in the inner ears. Dancers and gymnasts develop very good integration of body and gravity sensations so that their movements become graceful. Artists and craftspeople rely upon integration of their eye and hand sensations. People who are calm and happy are usually that way because of good nervous system integration. Most of us get by with an average amount of sensory integration.

The genes of the human species give us our baseline capacity for sensory integration. Although every child is born with this capacity, he must develop sensory integration by interacting with many things in the world and adapting his body and brain to many physical challenges during childhood. The greatest development of sensory integration occurs during an *adaptive response*.

Adaptive Responses

An adaptive response is a purposeful, goal-directed response to a sensory experience. A baby sees a rattle and reaches for it. Reaching is an adaptive response. Merely waving the hands about aimlessly is not adaptive. A more complex adaptive response occurs when the child perceives that the rattle is too far away and crawls to get it. In an adaptive response, we master a challenge and learn something new. At the same time, the formation of an adaptive response helps the brain to develop and organize itself. Most adults see this as merely play. However, play consists of the adaptive responses that make sensory integration happen. The child who learns to organize his play is more likely to organize his school work and become an organized adult.

A Sensory Processing Machine

Until about the age of seven, the brain is primarily a *sensory processing machine*. This means that it senses things and gets meaning directly from sensations. A young child doesn't have many thoughts or ideas about things; he is concerned mainly with sensing them and moving his body in relationship to those sensations. His adaptive responses are more muscular, or *motor*, than mental. Thus the first seven years of life are called the years of sensory-motor development.

As the child grows older, mental and social responses replace some of this sensory-motor activity. However, the brain's mental and social functions are based upon a foundation of sensory-motor processes. The sensory integration that occurs in moving, talking, and playing is the groundwork for the more complex sensory integration that is necessary for reading, writing, and good behavior. If sensory-motor processes are well organized in the first seven years of life, the child will have an easier time learning mental and social skills later on.

Having Fun

When the sensory integrative capacity of the brain is sufficient to meet the demands of the environment, the child's response is efficient, creative, and satisfying. When the child experiences challenges to which he can respond effectively, he "has fun." To some extent, "fun" is the child's word for sensory integration. It gives us a great deal of satisfaction to organize sensations, and even more satisfaction to respond to those sensations with adaptive responses that are more mature or more complex than anything we have done before. This is what growing up is all about.

A human being is designed to enjoy things that promote the development of his brain, and therefore we naturally seek sensations that help organize our brain. This is one of the reasons why children love to be picked up, rocked, and hugged, and why they love to run and jump and play at playgrounds and at the beach. They want to move because the sensations of movement nourish their brains.

Poor Sensory Integration Is . . .

Sensory integration is not an either/or matter. We don't have perfect sensory integration or none at all. None of us organizes sensations perfectly. Happy, productive, well-coordinated people may come the closest to perfect sensory integration. Some people have good sensory integration, others just average, and others poor.

If the brain does a poor job of integrating sensations, this will interfere with many things in life. There will be more effort and difficulty, and less success and satisfaction. About five to 10 percent of the children in this country today have enough trouble with sensory integration to cause them to be slow learners or to have behavior problems. However, these children usually seem normal in every way, and they often have average or above average intelligence.

Diagnosis

At present, there is no way to measure the disorder in the brain as it occurs. A sensory integrative disorder is not like a medical problem. Chemical imbalances, virus infections, blood irregularities, and tissue pathologies can be measured in the laboratory. A sensory integrative problem cannot be isolated so easily. We can only watch the child, both in his normal movements and sensory integration diagnostic tests, and try to judge how his brain is functioning. Only a trained observer can see the subtle differences between behavior that is based on good sensory integration and that which is based on poor integration.

Most physicians will test the child with medical procedures and then tell the parents that nothing is wrong. When the problem is not severe, parents often do not realize that something is wrong until the child goes to school and has trouble learning to read or write. If the mother has had other children, or is very intuitive, she may notice that something is not quite right with her child, but she usually can't say what it is. She may ask herself, "How can he be so much trouble if there is nothing wrong?" or "Why does he cry so easily?" or "Why is he so stubborn?" An occupational therapist or physical therapist who is trained in sensory integration can help answer these questions.

Some Early Symptoms

Some infants with sensory integrative problems do not roll over, creep, sit, or stand at the same age as other children. Later on they may have trouble learning to tie their shoes or ride a bicycle without training wheels. But other infants with poor sensory integration seem to develop on schedule, and only have trouble later on. They may not move easily or gracefully. Running may be awkward. They may seem clumsy and frequently fall or stumble. Not all clumsiness is caused by poor sensory integration, however; some people are clumsy because certain motor nerves or muscles do not work well. In the child with sensory integrative dysfunction, the nerves and muscles work all right, but the brain has trouble putting it all together.

Before going to school, the child with poor sensory integration may not play as skillfully as other children. Because he cannot integrate the information from his eyes and ears and hands and body, he may see or hear or feel something, but not respond adaptively to it. You may notice that he misses details or doesn't understand the way other children do. He may not choose the kind of playthings that are popular with other children; toys that require manipulation may be too much of a challenge. He may break things and have accidents more often than usual.

A delay in language development is a common problem and an early clue that all is not well in the brain. Some children do not listen well, although they do not have a hearing problem; it is as though the words entered their ears, but got lost on their way through the brain. Other children know what they want to say, but cannot direct their mouths to form the words.

Without clear messages from the hands and eyes, a child cannot color between the lines, put a puzzle together, cut accurately with scissors, or paste two pieces of paper together neatly. In every little task, he does more poorly than his peers. For him, the task is more difficult and more confusing. Adults may think that he is just not interested, but he has no interest because his sensations and his responses to them do not provide him meaning and satisfaction.

Some children cannot organize the sensations from their skin. They may get angry or anxious when people touch them, or even stand nearby. Much of the hyperactivity in children today is due to poor sensory integration. Sometimes lights or noises will irritate and distract the child; if you watch closely, you will notice the irritation in the child's face.

Problems in School

Sometimes the child does everything all right at home, or at least well enough that the problem is not noticed, but has great difficulty learning in school. Educators often call reading, writing, and arithmetic the "basics," but actually these are extremely complex processes that can develop only upon a strong foundation of sensory integration. A sensory integrative problem that is "minor" in early childhood may become a major handicap when the child enters school.

Parents and teachers expect more of a school-age child than they do of a younger child. Not only must the child learn a wide variety of new things, but he must also get along with many classmates and teachers. The brain that does not organize sensations well is also apt to have trouble making friends and keeping them. School puts the child under a lot of stress, for he has to work harder to do the same tasks as his classmates. Many children with poor sensory integration feel helpless and anxious in school.

There are a lot of little things that a child has to do in school. Without good sensory integration, it is hard to learn how to tie shoelaces, hold onto a pencil, not break the lead of the pencil, change from one task to another, recognize stop signs on the way to school, and so on. The child has to compete in sports with children having much better sensory-motor abilities. He has to pay attention in a roomful of people, although he can barely pay attention when alone with his teacher. He is expected to do things fast when he can only do them slowly, or do them slowly when it is easier to move quickly. He has to remember instructions to do two things at once—such as "Put away your books and then get out your pencil"— when it is hard to remember even a single instruction.

In the classroom he is easily distracted by all the extraneous sounds, lights, and the confusion of many people doing different things. His brain is overly stimulated and it responds with a lot of excessive activity. The hyperactive child "jumps all over the classroom," not because that is what he wants to do, but because his brain is running out of control. His excess activity is a compulsive reaction to sensations he can neither turn off nor organize. The confusion within his brain makes it impossible to focus or concentrate, and so he can't understand what his teacher is teaching. If he is standing in line and someone accidentally bumps into him, he may become angry or strike back. The anger and hitting have nothing to do with interpersonal relationships; they are automatic reactions to sensations the child cannot tolerate.

The child is not able to talk about these problems, nor can he understand what is going on, since the problem occurs in brain processess that are below consciousness and control. It is useless to tell him to control himself or concentrate harder. Rewards—such as candy or gold stars—and punishment do not make it easier for the brain to organize sensations. Adults often make the child's problem worse by making demands he cannot handle.

After a couple of years of these experiences, the child notices that he is different. He may realize that in some ways he will always be different. Without careful parental support, he is apt to grow up thinking that he is stupid or bad, especially since other children tell him that he is. It is not enough to tell him in words that he is not stupid or bad. Words and thoughts cannot organize the brain. Only sensations and adaptive responses can build his self-esteem.

A sensory integrative dysfunction is a heavy burden for anyone to carry.

Remember that every child with poor sensory integration shows a different set of symptoms. Even normal children show a few of these problems at one time or another. It is only when a child has many of these problems, and they occur much of the time, that parents should be concerned. If you think that your child has a sensory integrative problem, take him to an occupational or physical therapist trained in sensory integration procedures. (See Chapter 11.) With the help of therapy and parents who understand and give support, your child will probably be able to lead a normal life, enjoy social interactions, and make a contribution to society, although his personal development will probably never be optimal. If you think about all the adults you know, you will realize that everyone has some trouble learning and adapting. We all get along without perfect sensory integration.

Why Was This Book Written?

We hope that this book will help parents recognize sensory integrative problems in their children, understand what is going on, do something to help the child, and then understand what the sensory integration therapist is doing for the child. For this, you must think in terms of sensations from the body and from gravity, as well as the sensations from the eyes and ears, and of a brain that organizes these sensations and uses them to direct the body and mind. In addition, you must observe children and see what they like to do and how they do it. In the beginning you will notice only a few aspects of sensory integration; later on, you will see many more. Even after many years of observing this process in children, sensory integration therapists continue to notice new aspects of sensory integrative dysfunction.

In the next chapter, we shall look at the activities of normal infants and children and see how sensory integration develops. In Chapter 3, we discuss the brain, because that is where the problem occurs and that is what therapy changes. In Chapters 4–9 we explain the different types of sensory integrative disorder in detail. Chapter 10 is about what happens in sensory integrative therapy. The final chapter will help you at home to help your child's nervous system.

CHAPTER 2

WATCHING SENSORY INTEGRATION DEVELOP

In his first seven years, a child learns to sense his body and the world around him and to rise up and move effectively in that world. He learns what different sounds mean and how to speak. He learns how to interact with the physical forces of this planet, along with innumerable pieces of furniture, clothes, shoes, eating utensils, toys, pencils, books, and of course other people. Each of these gives him some sensory information and he must develop sensory integration to use that information and interact effectively.

Sensory integrative functions develop in a natural order, and every child follows the same basic sequence. Some children develop faster and some more slowly, but all travel pretty much the same path. Children who deviate a great deal from the normal sequence of sensory integrative development are apt to have trouble later on with other aspects of life.

In this chapter, we describe the major steps in sensory integrative development as we see them in normal children. You do not need professional qualifications to see how a child organizes his sensory-motor processes. All you need to do is look at him and other children during the day. You cannot see the brain, but you can see behaviors that reflect the activity of the brain.

Basic Principles of Child Development

There are certain basic principles that we see again and again in every child. The most basic principle deals with organization. Most of the activity in the first seven years of life is part of one process: the process of organizing the sensations in the nervous system.

A newborn infant sees and hears and senses his body, but he cannot organize these sensations well, and so most of them don't mean very much to him. He can't tell how far away things are, or what noises mean, or feel the shape of things in his hand, or know where his body is in relationship to everything else. As the child experiences sensations, he gradually learns to organize them within his brain and find out what they mean. He learns to focus his attention on particular sensations and ignore others. Movements that were clumsy and jerky in infancy become smoother and more direct in childhood. He learns the complicated movements of speech. By organizing sensations, the child gains control over his emotions. He learns to stay organized for longer periods of time. Some of the situations that upset an infant give an older child knowledge and satisfaction.

Organization through Adaptive Responses

The greatest sensory-motor organization occurs during an adaptive response to sensation. This is a response in which the person deals with his body and the environment in a creative or useful way. We hear a sound and turn our head to see what happened. Someone bumps into us and we shift our weight to regain our balance. Lay an infant on his tummy, and he lifts up his head and turns it to the side so that he can breathe more easily. For the older child, putting on clothes, playing with toys, and riding a bicycle require many adaptive responses.

We adapt to sensations. Before our body can make an adaptive response, we must organize the sensations from our body and from our environment. We can adapt to a situation only if our brain knows what the situation is. When a child acts in an adaptive manner, we know that his brain is organizing sensations efficiently.

In addition, each adaptive response leads to further integration of sensations that arise from making that response. A well-organized adaptive response leaves the brain in a more organized state. To integrate sensations, a child will try to adapt to those sensations. A child on a swing will move his body in response to sensations of gravity and movement, and his movements help his brain to organize those sensations. Nobody can make an adaptive response for the child; he must do it himself. Fortunately children are designed to enjoy activities that challenge them to experience new sensations and develop new motor functions. It is fun to integrate sensations and form adaptive responses.

Watch a child ride a bicycle and you will see how sensory stimulation leads to adaptive responses and adaptive responses lead to sensory integration. To balance himself and the bicycle, the child must sense the pull of gravity and the movements of his body. Whenever he moves off center and begins to fall, his brain integrates the sensations of falling and forms an adaptive response. In this case, the adaptive response involves shifting the weight of the body to keep it balanced over the bicycle. If this adaptive response is not made, or is made too slowly, the child falls off the bicycle. If he repeatedly cannot make the adaptive response because he does not get good, precise information from his body and gravity senses, he may avoid riding a bicycle.

Additional adaptive responses are needed to steer the bicycle so that it goes where the child wants it to go. To know where he and the bicycle are in relation to a tree, his brain must integrate visual sensations with body sensations and the pull of gravity. Then it must use those sensations to plan a path around the tree. The faster the bicycle goes, the greater the sensory stimulation and the more accurate the adaptive responses must be. If the child rides into a tree, it means that his brain did not integrate the sensations, or it did not do so quickly enough. When a child gets off his bicycle after a successful ride, his brain knows more about gravity and the space around his body and how his body moves, and so riding a bicycle becomes easier each time. This is how sensory integration develops.

The Inner Drive

Within every child, there is a great inner drive to develop sensory integration. We do not have to tell him to crawl or stand up or climb; nature directs the child from within. Watch how a child searches his environment for opportunities to develop and how he tries over and over again until he succeeds. Without this inner drive toward sensory integration, none of us could have developed. Because the inner drive is so great, we take most aspects of sensory-motor development for granted. Nature takes care of them automatically.

Building Blocks

In the sequence of development, the child uses each activity to develop "building blocks" that become the basis for more complex and more mature developments. He is constantly putting his functions together to form more organized functions. He practices an activity over and over to master each sensory and motor element. Sometimes he backs up and practices an earlier developmental step before going on to something new. It is easy to see the building blocks that lead to walking: holding the head upright must come before sitting, and creeping on all fours before walking on two legs. Although it is much harder to see, the senses also develop in sequences of building blocks. First the child develops the senses that tell him about his own body and its relationship to the gravitational field of the earth, and then these become the building blocks that help him to develop the senses of sight and sound, which tell him about things that are distant from his body. The visual perception involved in reading is the end product of many building blocks that form during the sensory-motor activities of infancy and early childhood. The same is true for all academic abilities and also for behavior and emotional growth; everything rests upon a sensory-motor foundation.

Now let us trace the major steps in the path of sensory integration. We shall follow them from the first month after birth up to age seven.

The Developmental Steps

The First Month

Touch. A newborn infant can already interpret some of his body sensations and respond with built-in reflex movements. His sense of touch has been operating fairly well for several months in the womb. If you gently touch his cheek, he is likely to turn his head toward your hand. This reflex is an adaptive reaction that nature designed to help infants find a meal. Place a cloth over his face as he lies on his back, and he will try to get it off by moving his head and arms. Although these innate reactions are automatic, the sensations must be integrated for the reflex to occur in a meaningful and purposeful way.

The sensations from a wet diaper make the infant uncomfortable, while the touch of his mother's hand is comforting. However, the child cannot tell very well where he is being touched, because his brain cannot differentiate one spot from another. At this age, touch sensations are more important as a source of emotional satisfaction. The touching between an infant and his mother is essential for brain development and the development of the mother-child bond.

During his first month, a baby will automatically grasp any object that touches the palm of his hand. This reflex is designed to help the child hang onto something so that he doesn't fall. Because the newborn does not have the ability to open or extend his fingers, his hands often remain curled into loose fists for the first few months of life.

Gravity and movement. The newborn also shows responses to the sensations of gravity and movement that come from his inner ears. If you hold him in your arms and suddenly lower him a foot or so, he will show alarm and his arms and legs may move outward as though to grasp something. The messages from his inner ears tell him that he is falling and that he better try to do something to protect himself. This clinging or flexion movement of the entire body is the first total-body motor pattern.

You might think that a human infant does not need automatic reactions to protect himself and find a meal since his mother takes care of him. However, these reflexes evolved in lower animals that needed them for infant survival. Evolution occurs very slowly and nature does not readily give up a form of behavior that has served survival for millions of years. Thus the operations of our nervous system are based upon the needs of the lower animals from which man evolved, and also the needs of man before he became civilized. These built-in responses provide building blocks for the development of more advanced abilities.

When the one-month-old child is held up with his head resting on his parent's shoulder, he will intermittently try to lift up his head. This happens because the pull of gravity stimulates the part of the brain that, in turn, activates the neck muscles that raise the head. Over the next few weeks, this adaptive response will develop so that the baby can lift his head while lying on his stomach. The same neural mechanism holds an adult's head upright without deliberate effort. At one month, however, it is still immature and the infant's head wobbles and needs support.

Every mother quickly learns that carrying or rocking a child brings him comfort and usually quiets him. The sensations of gentle body movement tend to organize the brain, and this is why the image of a cradle brings back so many fond memories. In addition to calming the baby, carrying and rocking provide sensations that are essential building blocks for other sensations and for self-determined body movements. Although you cannot actually see this happening in the brain, you can easily see that your child wants to be carried and rocked. Sensations that make a child happy tend to be integrating.

Muscle and joint sensations. The average one-month-old child will adjust his body to fit nicely into the arms and body of the person holding him. He senses how to do this through his muscles and joints. Later on his muscles and joints will tell him how to use a knife and fork and how to climb a Jungle gym. The child must practice and organize many, many movements to develop adult skills. In his first few months, therefore, the infant makes many movements that appear random and haphazard, and then later on become well organized. When lying on his back he thrusts his arms and legs out playfully. On his stomach he makes alternating crawling motions. These movements occur because the sensations from his muscles and joints and inner ears stimulate his nervous system to produce movements. Meanwhile the child's inner drive helps him to organize these sensations and movements.

Muscle and joint sensations also tell the brain when the head is turned to one side. This activates a reaction known as the *tonic neck reflex*, which makes the arm on that side tend to extend or straighten while the other arm tends to bend at the elbow. Notice the words *tends to*. This is only a tendency; it does not always happen when the infant's head is turned. During the first few weeks of life, this reflex plays a major role in determining arm movements; and so the infant lying on his back often looks toward his extended arm while his other arm is bent. Although the tonic neck reflex influences the muscle tone in our arms for our entire life, its influence should become negligible by the sixth year. In children with poor sensory integration, the reflex is often overactive. Occupational and physical therapists often look for overactive tonic neck reflex responses as a sign of poor sensory integration.

Sight. The one-month-old infant's sense of sight is not very well organized, although he does recognize his mother's face and other significant objects. His focus is vague and he cannot differentiate complex shapes or color contrasts. He can sense danger in movement or in touch, but not from sight. His first step in developing vision is to learn to follow a moving object or person with his eyes and then his head. This adaptive response requires sensations from the muscles surrounding the eyes and in the neck, in conjunction with gravity and movement sensations from the inner ears. Notice how an infant becomes alert and happy when he sees movement in people or animals or toys, and can practice his ability to follow them with his eyes.

Sound. The one-month-old child will respond to the sound of a rattle or bell, and also to the human voice, although he cannot understand what these sounds mean. He may turn his head or smile. Simply responding to sounds is the first building block in the development of speech. He also makes small throaty sounds. The muscular contractions in the throat that cause these sounds also produce sensations that help to develop speech areas of the brain.

Smell and taste. Another sense that is probably well organized at birth is the sense of smell. It may play an important role during the first month of life. Like the senses of gravity, movement, and touch, this sense appeared early in the evolution of animals from which man evolved. The sense of smell is not further developed and refined in the older child in the way that sight and hearing are. The infant can also taste well. Sucking is the adaptive response that comes from taste and smell, and the infant usually has the reflex when he is born.

So at one month, the infant has already performed a considerable number of adaptive responses to sensations, particularly to the sensations from his own body and from gravity. Many of these responses are built into his nervous system before birth, so that they would be turned on by the sensations of gravity and movement and touch. Without the integration that occurs in this simple sensory-motor activity, adequate development would be impossible later on in life.

The Second and Third Months

The eyes and neck. The infant's motor functions develop from head to toe. The eyes and neck are the first body parts he learns to control. Keeping the head and eyes stable is a fundamental ability that has very important survival value. Visual perception involves more than just looking at something; in addition, the eyes must hold a steady image of the object and the neck must keep the head steady, otherwise the object would appear to blur and flutter, like a photograph taken by a camera that is not held steady. For this, the brain must integrate three types of sensation: one, the gravity and movement sensations from the inner ears; two, the sensations from the eye muscles; and three, the muscle sensations from the neck. The brain puts these three types of sensation together to know how to hold the eyes and neck steady.

As the infant scans the room and looks at people and objects, his brain is busy working to integrate the sensations from his inner ears, eye muscles, and neck muscles. Through this integrative process, he learns to "take a clear picture" of his environment even when his head or even his whole body is moving. This development will continue for several years and is a vital building block for learning to read. It also helps the child learn balance and overall body movement.

Rising up. When you think of how consistent and powerful gravity is, you realize how much inner drive the child must have to rise to a standing position in just one year. After he learns to hold his head up with his neck muscles, the infant uses the muscles in his upper back and arms to lift his chest off the floor. This development occurs in the prone position (lying face downward). The infant's urge to lift his chest comes mainly from the sensations of gravity, which stimulate the brain to contract the muscles in the upper back. The child also learns to sit upright with his head balanced if you support his lower back. Some challenge is necessary for any learning. Supporting his entire back eliminates the challenge, while giving no support to the lower back makes the challenge too great for the child at this age.

Grasping. The three-month-old infant's hands are open most of the time. He reaches for objects and people but lacks the eye-hand coordination necessary to make his reach accurate. As he integrates body sensations with what he sees, he finds out how to aim properly.

When he grabs, he does not use his thumb and forefinger; instead he holds the objects with his three other fingers and the palm of his hand. He grasps a rattle in this simple way, and his sense of touch sends messages to his brain that help him to hold onto the object. At this age, grasping is still an automatic reaction to the touch sensations in the palm of his hand, and he cannot voluntarily release his hold on the rattle. Over the next few months he will integrate these touch sensations with the sensations from the muscles and joints in his hands and gradually develop a more efficient pincer motion with his thumb and fingers.

The Fourth to Sixth Months

The arms and hands. Now the baby makes big movements, such as banging a spoon against a table, and experiences the thrill of having an impact on the physical world. This very simple emotional satisfaction is a building block toward the more mature emotions that develop later on.

He now begins to touch and look at his hands, and thereby develop an awareness of where his hands are in space. He needs touch and muscle and joint sensations along with vision to learn to use his hand accurately in conjunction with what he sees. He has to coordinate the parts of his brain that "see" with those parts that "feel" the hand and arm. He begins to use his thumb and forefinger, but his grip lacks precision. He is apt to reach with one hand more often than with both together since he can now control his urge to reach.

One of the most important developments of this age occur when the child spontaneously brings his hands together in front of his body so that they touch each other. This is the beginning of coordination between the two sides of the body. Another step in this development occurs a few months later when he holds a toy in each hand and bangs them together. These actions require an important type of sensory integration that must develop long before the child can know his right and left. Infants who do not touch their hands together and bang toys are more likely to show signs of poor sensory integration when they are older.

By his sixth month, the child's wrist rotates so he can turn his hand and manipulate objects and play in many new ways. Most of the movements in the first six months were automatic, but now the infant begins to do things that he must plan. Each new play activity involves more of this "motor planning" and more sensory integration. He can also sit alone for a short time without losing his balance. The automatic muscular reactions that keep him upright are guided by the sensations of gravity, movement, and sight. If these sensations are not well integrated, the infant will have difficulty sitting or may not even try to sit.

The airplane position. At about six months, the infant's nervous system becomes particularly sensitive to the pull of gravity on his head while he is lying on his stomach. This sensitivity produces a strong urge to raise the head, upper back, arms, and legs all at the same time. The baby balances his whole body on his stomach, and looks a little bit like an airplane. Therapists refer to this as the *prone extension posture*. This position is a vital step in developing the muscles that are used for rolling over, standing up, and walking. Older children who cannot hold this position often have problems integrating gravity and movement sensations.

The joy of being moved. The six-month-old child also likes to be rocked, held up, swung in the air, turned over, and moved about. These are among the most satisfying experiences of infancy. The joy comes from experiencing stronger gravity and movement sensations, which the child can now integrate. If the movements are too rough or the child cannot integrate the sensations, they will disorganize his nervous system and cause him to cry.

The Sixth to Eight Months

Locomotion. One of the most important aspects of development during this period is locomotion, or movement from one place to another. Locomotion greatly increases the number of things and places the infant can explore. Crawling and creeping on hands and knees contribute many sensations to be integrated and also give the child a concept of himself an an independent being.

First he must get himself into the prone position, on his stomach. A reflex known as the "neck righting reflex," which has been active since birth, helps him turn over from his back to his stomach. This is the same reflex that enables a cat to land on his feet even when he is dropped with his back down and feet up. The sensations that activate this reflex come from gravity and the muscles and joints of the neck. These sensations activate the neck righting reflex for much of the time at this age, and so the normal infant tends to spend a lot of time lying on his stomach.

Spatial perception. Locomotion gives the child knowledge about space and the distance between himself and objects in the environment. It is not enough merely to see things to judge distance; the brain must also "feel" the nature of distance through the sensations of body movement. As he crawls and creeps from one place to another, he learns the physical structure of space, and this helps him to understand what he sees. Good distance judgment also helps the child to know how large things are. If the child at this age has difficulty integrating the sensations of crawling and creeping, he may later on have trouble judging distance and size.

The fingers and eyes. The child can now use his thumb and forefinger in a scissors or pincer action to pick up small objects or pull a string. He can also poke his forefinger in a hole. The sensations of touch, and those from his muscles and joints, provide the basic information and guides these movements. For fine hand motions, however, he needs precise information from his eyes. He must have fine control over his eye muscles to direct his eyes precisely to the place he needs to see. To develop precise eye control, the child must already have the simple eye control that developed as he lay on his stomach and raised his head, crawled, and crept about in his environment.

Motor planning. At this age, the child begins to plan his hand movements well enough to ring a bell or put simple things together and take them apart. Movements must be planned inside the brain to complete a sequence of actions in the proper order. Sensations from the body provide the information necessary for planning movements.

This is also the age when the child begins to look for an object that has been covered up or dropped out of sight. By touching and moving around objects, he learns that they still exist even when he cannot see them. This is the beginning of the mental ability to visualize objects.

Babbling. The eight-month-old child listens to sounds well enough to hear details. He recognizes familiar words and knows that some sounds mean one thing and others mean something else. He may repeat simple syllables such as "ma" and "da," although this is not really speech. Babbling sends sensations from the jaw joint, muscles, and skin of the mouth to the brain. As the brain integrates more and more of these sensations, it learns how to form more complex sounds. If the child has difficulty with babbling, he may have trouble learning to speak.

The Ninth to Twelfth Months

This is the time for major changes in the way the child relates to the earth and the space around his body. He creeps for longer distances and explores more places in his environment. This stimulates his nervous system with many sensations from the muscles that hold up his head and body and the bones that support his weight, and also from the pull of gravity. These sensations help him coordinate the two sides of his body, learn how to motor plan, and develop visual perception. He spends a lot of time just looking at things and figuring out what they are. The more different things he experiences as he roams about, the more practice he gets in integrating sensations and forming adaptive responses to those sensations.

Play. Watch your child banging things together, pulling them off a table, throwing them about, and so on, and try to see the importance of what he is doing and sensing. Very often one of his hands reaches across to the other side of his body. These motions develop his ability to *cross the midline*, a very important ability that is sometimes poor in children with sensory integrative dysfunctions. Every time he puts something together or takes it apart, his brain learns to plan and carry out a sequence of movements in proper order. Every time he makes a mess of his food with a spoon or scribbles with a crayon, he learns something about tools and how to use them.

Standing up. One of the biggest events in early childhood is standing up alone. Few adults can ever realize the significance of this magnificent achievement and what it means to the child's self-concept. It is the end product of all the integration of gravity, movement, and muscle and joint sensations of the months before. Standing up requires the integration of sensations from every part of the body, including the eye and neck muscles, which continue to be essential. Standing up is quite a challenge since a relatively tall body must balance itself on two small feet. It is best to allow the child to practice standing up on his own, so that he masters that challenge by himself.

Words. The child can now understand a fair amount of what his parents say, but can speak only a few simple words like "mama" and "dada." It appears that the sensations arising from body movement help to stimulate the part of the brain that is involved in making these sounds.

The Second Year

Now the child learns to walk, to talk, and to plan more complex actions and perform them more effectively. It is quite certain that without all the sensory integration that took place during the first year, it would be very difficult for the child to learn these things. And in turn, without the integration that occurs in this second year, all subsequent development would be difficult.

Localization of touch. The ability to plan movements depends upon the accuracy of the child's touch system. At birth, the infant knew that he was touched and touch affected his emotional state, but he did not know where he was touched. He moved his head in response to the touch, but this was an automatic reflex reaction rather than a consciously directed action. By his second year, he can tell roughly where he is touched, and also direct his responses somewhat voluntarily. We can see that touch sensations make it feel good to hold things; they tell the brain something about those things that seeing does not tell. The sensations from his skin also tell him where his body begins and where it ends. This sensory awareness of the body is far more basic than visual knowledge of the body.

Children who cannot integrate these sensations well are not able to feel exactly how their bodies are structured or what each part is doing. Therefore they have trouble learning to do things. They may learn to sit, stand, and walk all right, but have trouble playing with toys or using buttons, zippers, and kitchen utensils. If you see a child fumble around with things or drop them more often than other children his age, he is probably not getting good, precise touch information from his hands.

Moving. During this year, the child practices countless variations of movement to gain additional sensory awareness of how his body functions and how the physical world operates. He picks up things and throws them, pushes and pulls toys, walks up and down stairs, explores his home and the world outdoors, and gets into everything, often to his parents' distress. However, parents should be more distressed if the child does not get into everything. A child needs opportunities to interact with the physical environment as much as he needs food and love.

Mapping the body. Children at this age enjoy rough-housing, piggyback rides, and swinging. These activities provide a lot of sensory input from the body and from the gravity receptors in the inner ears. They give him a feeling of how gravity works, how the different parts of his body move, how they interact with each other, what they cannot do, what feels good, and what hurts or feels uncomfortable. All of this sensory information forms an internal sensory "picture" of the body inside the brain. We shall call this a *body percept*. To understand the body percept, it may be helpful to think of a world atlas that contains maps of every part of the world. As the child moves and experiences the consequences of his movement, he "maps out" his body. His brain stores countless bits of information that he can later use to "navigate" his body movements.

Climbing. Children have an inner drive to explore space not only horizontally, but also vertically. Children climb some things even before they walk. In order to climb, the child must have well-organized gravity and movement sensations, and climbing further integrates these with body sensations and also visual information. Climbing requires a great deal of "sensory-motor intelligence" and is an important step toward the development of visual space perception.

Two-year-olds also learn to understand and follow directions and instructions. Most children learn to say a number of things during this year; others wait until the following year for their major speech development.

Selfhood. If the sensations from the child's body are making him feel like a secure and competent individual—a being separate and distinct from his mother and every other person and thing—then he is well on his way to developing a satisfactory self-concept. Establishing *selfhood* becomes an important task as the child approaches the age of two. He is an individual person, because he feels his body as a physical whole and can move well by himself. He is no longer a slave to gravity; he can stand upright, walk long distances, go up and down hills, jump and climb. He can hide and reappear because he knows the dimensions of his body, and peek-a-boo is an important activity at this age. By having an impact on his environment, he furthers his sense of self; and so he enjoys pulling pots and pans out of cupboards, knocking things over, and making marks with crayons and paint.

As he approaches his second birthday, he begins to feel that he can be in command of his own life, and he lets others know this. Many children at this age use the word "no" to express their new-found independence. This may be frustrating to parents, but it is a necessary stage in the development of social skills. It takes a lot of patience and wisdom to accept the child's need to resist his parents' wishes.

The child can be in command of his life only to the extent that his body sensations allow him to move freely and effectively. His life is still mostly feeling and moving, in addition to eating, sleeping, and relating to family members. The integration of sensations provides the foundation for good relations with people. If a child behaves poorly with other people, this may be a reflection of his inability to deal with sensations.

Although the child has taken the first steps toward being a self-reliant person, he is still a long way from being on his own. He needs a great deal of support, encouragement, and comfort. A lot of this comes from being hugged, held in someone's lap, rocked, cuddled, and kissed. Comforting sensations are integrating, and they help to organize a child when he is temporarily disorganized.

The Third through Seventh Years

During these five years, the child becomes a mature sensory-motor being who can talk and relate to many different people. Higher intellectual functions will develop after age seven, and they will develop better if the sensory-motor functions are well developed. The third through seventh years are a critical period for sensory integration. Nature intended this to be the time when the brain is most receptive to sensations and most able to organize them. The child's inner drive makes him very active and he learns to do many, many things with his body. His adaptive responses are more and more complex, and each adaptive response expands the child's capacity for sensory integration.

Watch a child run, jump, hop, skip, roll, wrestle, climb, and swing. He does these things because they are fun; and they are fun because they further sensory integration. Notice the improvements in balance, eye-hand coordination, and planning of a sequence of movements. Notice how the child tries things that are dangerous so that he learns the limits of his sensory-motor ability. Notice how he pits himself against gravity and comes to terms with that powerful and unforgiving force. Playgrounds are popular with children because swings, slides, merry-go-rounds, monkey bars, see-saws, tunnels, and sandboxes fulfill the needs of the developing nervous system.

Using tools. Between the ages of three and seven, a child learns to use simple tools such as knives, forks, shovels, pails, needle and thread, scissors, crayons, pencil and paper, shoelaces, zippers, buttons, and all the other devices that make up a home. Each task requires all the sensory information that has been stored in the brain during earlier activities. Adults take it for granted, but sensations from the body are absolutely necessary to tell the brain how to put on a pair of pants, butter a piece of bread, or dig a hole in the ground.

Toward the end of this period we see, especially in girls, a final "polishing" of motor skills through complex games such as hopscotch, pease porridge hot, hula-hooping, jump rope, and cat's cradle. Boys usually work more on feats of strength and sports.

By the time the child is eight years old, his touch system is almost as mature as it will ever be. He can almost always tell with great accuracy where he is being touched. His sense of gravity and movement is also almost fully mature. He can balance himself on one foot and walk a narrow surface. Most of the sensations from his muscles and joints should be well-integrated, and his ability to plan a sequence of actions is good, although it will improve in the next few years. He understands and speaks language well enough to communicate his needs and interests.

Jean Piaget, the famous observer of children, found that they do not begin abstract thinking and reasoning until they are seven or eight years old. Piaget suggested that the human brain is not designed to process abstractions until it has a "concrete" knowledge of the body, the world, and its physical forces. Seven or eight years of moving and play are required to give the child a sensory-motor intelligence that can serve as the foundation for intellectual, social, and personal development.

But sometimes this development does not occur the way nature intended. We cannot tell why things go wrong in a particular child, but we do know what the child is like when his brain has difficulty integrating sensations. We cannot take the place of nature and make everything all right, but we can do some things to help the child organize himself a little better. The ability to help a child organize his brain comes from watching children follow their own inner drive toward sensory integration. The more you watch your child, the more you will be able to help him.

REFERENCES

Piaget, Jean. *The origins of intelligence in children.* New York: W.W. Norton, 1952.

CHAPTER 3

THE NERVOUS SYSTEM WITHIN

The behaviors and academic learning of your child are the visible expression of the invisible activity within his nervous system. Learning and behavior are the visible aspects of sensory integration. To understand sensory integration more fully, you must know something about the structures and functions of the nervous system. This chapter will help you understand the neural processes that cause your child to learn and behave the way he does.

A Short Synopsis

The structures of the nervous system include two large cerebral hemispheres, a smaller cerebellum, a brain stem, a spinal cord, and a number of nerves that spread out to each part of the body. These structures are shown in Figure 1. Each of these structures contain many nerve cells, which are called *neurons*. Each neuron has a fiber that conducts electrical impulses along its length. The neurons that carry impulses from the body to or within the brain are called *sensory neurons*; the ones that carry impulses from the brain to the muscles and internal organs are called *motor neurons*.

The primary task of neurons is to tell us about our body and our environment, and to produce and direct our actions and thoughts. Each part of our body has sensory receiving organs, or *receptors*, that pick up energy from that body part just as a radio receiver picks up radio waves from the air. The receptors of the eyes pick up light waves; the receptors of the nose receive odors; and those of the muscles are sensitive to muscle contraction and stretching. Each receptor changes the energy into streams of electrical impulses that flow through sensory nerve fibers to the spinal cord and brain. The streams of electrical energy flowing toward the brain are called *sensory input*.

The spinal cord, brain stem, cerebellum, and cerebral hemispheres use the sensory input from the receptors to produce awareness, perception, and knowledge, and to produce body posture, movements, and the planning and coordination of movements, emotions, thoughts, memories, and learning. Over 80 percent of the nervous system is involved in processing or organizing sensory input, and thus the brain is primarily a *sensory process-ing machine*. Sensory processing is extremely complex since the different types of sensory input intermingle with each other throughout the entire brain. This very complex sensory processing produces a message in the brain, and the motor neurons then carry that message to the body. Each muscle receives many motor neurons, and the electrical impulses in the motor neurons cause the muscle to contract. Many muscle contractions must be combined to turn the eyes and head to look at something, or move the hands and fingers to manipulate an object, or move the body from one place to another.

For these muscle contractions to be coordinated and effective, the activity in the brain must be well organized. Sensory integration is the process of organizing sensory inputs so that the brain produces a useful body response and also useful perceptions, emotions, and thoughts. Sensory integration sorts, orders, and eventually puts all of the individual sensory inputs together into a whole brain function. When the functions of the brain are whole and balanced, body movements are highly adaptive, learning is easy, and good behavior is a natural outcome.

Now we shall discuss the structures and functions of the brain in greater detail.

The Parts of the Nervous System

The Neuron

This is the basic unit of the nervous system. There are about 12 billion (12,000,000,000) neurons in the average person. This number, more than three times the entire human population of this planet, gives us some idea of how complex neural functions are. Twelve billion is the number of seconds in 380 years.

Each neuron consists of a cell body and a fiber that divides into many branches and twig-like smaller fibers. Some of the "twigs" of one neuron connect to a number of points on other neurons. Most fibers have thousands of twigs, and that allows connection to thousands of other neurons. The branches and twigs of all these neurons intertwine like the twigs of trees in a dense forest, but with much greater complexity. The signals travel in only one direction in each neuron, but some of the impulses eventually may come back to act on the first neuron. The flow of electrical impulses through this complicated network produces our learning and behavior.

Nerve fibers conduct hundreds of impulses per second, and these impulses branch out and flow in many directions all at once. It has been estimated that in a single second, one impulse will spread out through up to a million neurons in many different parts of the brain. This is how a single sound or a touch on the finger can produce awareness, meaning, thoughts, emotions, learning, and behavior all in the same instant. The activity within your nervous system right now, and at every moment of life, is many times more complicated than any of us can imagine. Organizing that activity is quite a feat!

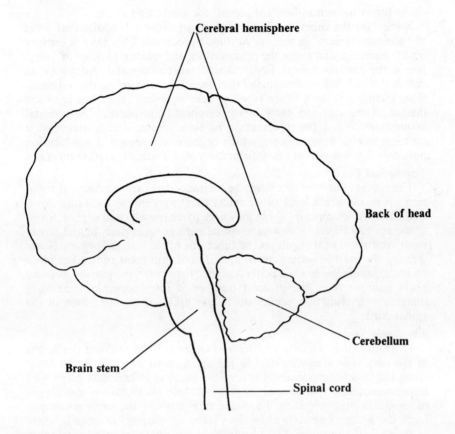

Cerebral hemisphere

Back of head

Cerebellum

Brain stem

Spinal cord

Figure 1. A View of the Brain as though it were Cut Down the Middle

As you read this book, imagine the awesome complexity of that world inside your head. As you watch your child struggle to learn how to tie his shoelaces or become overly excited at a birthday party, remember the countless streams of electrical impulses that are generating what you see.

Nerve Tracts and Nuclei

Many neurons are arranged in long thin bundles called nerve tracts. Most of these tracts carry one type of sensory input or motor response from one place in the nervous system to another place. Some carry more than one type of input. The orderly arrangement of these tracts prevents the information from being jumbled in somewhat the same way that most telephone lines carry each individual conversation separately. We have tracts for visual sensations, for sound, for smell, and so on.

Nuclei, on the other hand, are clusters of nerve cell bodies that serve as "business centers" in sensory or motor processes. They take in sensory input, rearrange and refine the information, and relate it to other information in the nervous system. For instance, visual information from the eyes passes through brain stem nuclei that rearrange and refine this information, integrate it with other types of sensory input, and then send the integrated messages to parts of the cerebral hemispheres. The cerebral hemispheres refine the information to even greater details and send it on to motor or other centers, which organize a response. Each location puts together many types of information into a more complete message.

The Spinal Cord

The spinal cord contains many nerve tracts that carry sensory information up to the brain, and other tracts that carry motor messages down to the nerves, which carry those messages to the muscles and organs. Some of the activity traveling down the spinal cord governs posture and movement, and some of it regulates the functions of the internal organs. Some sensory integration occurs in the spinal cord, but most of it takes place up in the brain. The brain is better designed for sensory integration, because brain neurons have the greatest number of interconnections. Sensory integrative dysfunction occurs up in the brain, then, not down in the spinal cord.

The Brain Stem

The brain stem is a small cylinder of neurons lying at about the height of the ears. The sensory tracts in the spinal cord continue in the brain stem, but in addition to these tracts, the brain stem contains many very important and complex nuclei. In many of these nuclei, two or more types of sensation come together. The brain stem is where the many sensations from the orange (mentioned in the preceding chapter) become a single experience of an orange. Most brain stem activity is automatic and takes place without our willing it or thinking about it.

The central core of the brain stem is a group of neurons and nuclei that may be compared to a tangled fishing net. Scientists who studied the nervous system under high-powered microscopes named this the *reticular formation*. The word "reticular" means net-like, and the reticular formation is even more complex and entangled than the rest of the brain. It contains fibers that connect it to every sensory system, to many motor neurons, and to most other parts of the brain. These connections enable the reticular formation to play a very important part in processing and integrating sensory-motor activities.

The brain stem reticular core contains the autonomic nuclei, which process information from the bloodstream and vital organs, and use this information to regulate heartbeat, breathing, and digestion. Other reticular nuclei act as "arousal centers" for the entire nervous system; these centers wake us up, calm us down, or excite us. Still other reticular nuclei play a major role in organizing the activities of the cerebral hemispheres, and this organization enables us to change our focus of attention from one thing to another. If reticular processes are not well organized, the person cannot focus his attention and daily events tend to overexcite him.

You are probably used to thinking of the brain as something that is "scientific" and foreign to your daily experience. One activity of the reticular formation offers a good example of a brain function you use every day. The reticular formation "turns up" in the morning as you awaken and "turns down" at night as you fall asleep. However, sensations are what turn the reticular formation up or down. In the morning, therefore, people wake themselves up with the sound of an alarm clock, cold water or a slap on the face, walking or jogging outdoors, or some other form of strong sensory stimulation. Sensation energizes the reticular formation and therefore arouses the entire brain. On the other hand, at night we want our reticular formation to turn down, so we lie motionless in a soft, warm bed in a dark, quiet room. The lack of stimulating sensations allows us to fall asleep.

Vestibular Nuclei and Cerebellum

The brain stem also contains a set of infinitely complex nuclei that process sensations from the gravity and movement receptors in the inner ears and use this information to maintain upright posture, equilibrium, and many other automatic functions. The vestibular nuclei in the brain stem also process a great deal of information for all of the other senses, especially the joint and muscle senses.

The cerebellum is wrapped around the back of the brain stem. Originally the cerebellum was an outgrowth of the vestibular nuclei, and so one of the functions of the cerebellum is an extension of what the vestibular nuclei do. The cerebellum processes all types of sensation, but is especially useful for organizing gravity, movement, and muscle-joint sensations to make our body movements smooth and accurate.

The Cerebral Hemispheres

Most of the mass of the brain consists of the two cerebral hemispheres, one on each side of the head. These hemispheres perform the most complex organizing of sensory input, including the processing that gives us the precise, detailed meaning of sensations. The cerebral hemispheres also include areas that are involved in planning and performing an action with the body. Also within the cerebral hemispheres is the *limbic system*, a set of neural structures that are involved in emotionally based behavior. These "emotional centers" receive sensory input that helps them regulate emotional responses and emotional growth.

The Cerebral Cortex

The outer layer of the cerebral hemispheres is called the *cerebral cortex*. The word "cortex" means "bark" in Latin. In humans, the cerebral cortex is highly specialized; there is one area for visual perceptions, another area for interpreting sounds from the environment, another for understanding speech, large areas for interpreting body sensations, and several areas for voluntary control of body and eye movements. The areas for body sensations and voluntary control of movements are divided into sections that deal with a particular part of the body. Although there are sections for every part of the body, the sections for the fingers, hands, and speech muscles are much larger than the sections for the rest of the body. Thus the cerebral cortex is especially important for sensing and directing precise, complex hand actions such as the use of a knife and fork or a pencil, and for speech.

While many of these cortical areas are specialized to interpret information from just one sense, each area also receives information from the other senses. For example, the visual area also processes some part of our sound, touch, and movement experiences. Very often the same cortical neuron will respond to two or more types of sensations and will not respond to just one type alone. In this way, the cerebral cortex continues the integration of all types of sensations and forms our associations between various types of sensation.

The cerebral cortex also contains *association areas*. The patterns of electrical activity in this area coordinate many different kinds of sensory experience into a unitary whole. Visual awareness forms in the brain stem and becomes precise in the visual areas of the cortex; the impulses then travel to the visual association areas where the visual information is associated with memories of other visual experiences, and then on to other association areas that form a mental evaluation and sometimes a voluntary response. When a child feels a puzzle piece, the touch sensations from his fingers are organized in the brain stem; the details are processed in the sensory areas of the cortex, and compared with other puzzle pieces in the association areas. All of this sensory processing then helps the brain choose what to do with that piece.

Because these cortical areas are so important in the highest levels of sensory processing, including the levels we are aware of in our thoughts, one is apt to think that a perceptual or learning problem occurs in the cerebral cortex. So far, neuro-scientific research has shown that the lower levels of the brain have a much more important role in these problems. The "higher" cortical organization depends upon the sensory organization at each of the lower levels. If the cortex is not working properly, the problem may well be that the lower levels are not doing their work well.

Lateralization

The two hemispheres do not do exactly the same things, nor do they do them the same way. Certain functions are specialized in one hemisphere. This is called *lateralization* from the Latin word for "side." The process of lateralization has been a topic of discussion among those concerned with speech and learning problems for many decades. Its role is not very well understood.

Sensory and motor functions are lateralized in early childhood. Most sensory and motor messages cross in the brain stem on their way to the cerebral hemispheres. Sensations from the right side of the body cross over to the left hemisphere, and the left hemisphere is the major source of control for the right side of the body. The right hemisphere handles the sensory processing and motor direction for the left side of the body.

Each hemisphere also specializes in particular functions. In right-handed persons, the left hemisphere is better at directing fine motor skills such as writing, and so the person writes with his right hand. This left hemisphere also produces language, while the right hemisphere deals more with the spatial relationships among visual and touch sensations. Some left-handed persons have the same lateralization of language as do right-handers, while others have the reverse. For complex functions, both hemispheres need to be involved and work together.

Good specialization of function usually leads to overall efficiency in brain processes, while poor specialization often slows down language development and academic learning. Good lateralization is probably the end product of normal brain growth and maturation. There are a number of different aspects of brain dysfunction that may contribute to poor lateralization.

Detailed spatial perception, language and speech, and cognitive thinking are among the most complex functions of the brain. They require very precise operations of the two sides of the brain, but the two sides can work well together only if the brain stem works well. Coordinated function of the two sides of the brain occurs automatically in most people without our being aware of it. However, when this coordination does not happen in a child or an adult, we see the effects in learning and behavior.

The Sensations

Sensations are "food" or nourishment for the nervous system. Every muscle, joint, vital organ, bit of skin, and sense organ in the head sends sensory inputs to the brain. Every sensation is a form of information. The nervous system uses this information to produce responses that adapt the body and mind to that information. Without a good supply of many kinds of sensations, the nervous system cannot develop adequately. The brain needs a continuous variety of sensory nourishment to develop and then to function.

In this section, we shall discuss the various types of sensation: first the senses which give us most of our conscious awareness of the world, and then the other senses, which we usually take for granted because they are processed semi-consciously in the brain.

Sight

The retina of the eye is a receptor that is sensitive to light waves in the environment. Light stimulates the retina to send visual sensory input to the visual processing centers in the brain stem. These centers process the impulses and relate them to other types of sensory information, especially input from the muscles and joints and vestibular system. This brain stem integration forms our basic awareness of the environment and the location of things in it.

The brain stem nuclei then send the impulses on to other parts of the brain stem and cerebellum to be integrated with motor messages going to muscles that move the eyes and neck. This is the neural process that enables us to follow a moving object with our eyes and head. Some of the impulses travel on to several different structures within the cerebral hemispheres for additional organization, refinement, and integration with other types of sensation. Some of the input reaches the visual areas of the cerebral cortex where fine, precise discrimination of visual details occurs—again with the help of information from the other senses. Proper functioning at all levels of the brain and integration of many types of sensation with the visual input are necessary to see meaning in the environment, especially on a piece of paper or the pages of a book.

Sound

Sound waves in the air stimulate the auditory receptors in the inner ear to send impulses to the brain stem auditory centers. These nuclei process the auditory impulses, along with impulses from the vestibular system and the muscles and skin. The auditory organizing centers are very close to the visual processing centers in the brain stem, and the two exchange information. Like the visual input, some of the auditory impulses travel to other parts of the brain stem and cerebellum for integration with other sensations and motor messages. The auditory information, which is now mixed in with other sensory information, then goes on to several parts of the cerebral hemispheres.

If the auditory information did not intermingle with other types of sensory information at each level of the brain, we would have trouble making meaning out of what we hear. A great deal of integration with vestibular and other inputs is needed to make the most sense out of the sounds. At each level in the brain, the message becomes clearer and more precise. The most intricate and complicated part of the process is the refinement of certain sounds into meaningful syllables and words.

Touch or the Tactile Sense

The skin has many different kinds of receptors for receiving sensations of touch, pressure, texture, heat or cold, pain, and movement of the hairs on the skin. Although we may not think much about the role of touch in our lives, the tactile system is the largest sensory system and it plays a vital role in human behavior, both physical and mental.

Touch receptors below the neck send impulses to the spinal cord and these impulses rise up to the brain stem. Receptors in the skin of the head send their impulses through cranial nerves directly to the brain stem. From the brain stem, tactile information is widely distributed throughout the rest of the brain. Many of these impulses never reach those parts of the cerebral cortex that makes us aware of the sensation. Instead these impulses are used at lower levels of the brain to help us move effectively, to adjust the reticular arousal system, to influence emotions, and to give meaning to other types of sensory information.

The nuclei in the brain stem that process tactile inputs can tell us that something is touching the skin, and whether that "something" is painful, cold, hot, wet, or scratchy. In general, the brain stem is designed to detect whether a stimulus is dangerous. However, these nuclei cannot tell us exactly where the stimulus is on the skin or what shape it is. Details of location and shape are processed in the sensory areas of the cerebral cortex.

Tactile impulses go just about everywhere in the brain. In addition, the tactile system is the first sensory system to develop in the womb and is able to function effectively when the visual and auditory systems are

just beginning to develop. For these reasons, touch is very important for
overall neural organization. Without a great deal of tactile stimulation of
the body, the nervous system tends to become "unbalanced."

Proprioception

The word *proprioception* refers to the sensory information caused
by contraction and stretching of muscles and by bending, straightening,
pulling, and compression of the joints between bones. Sheaths that cover
the bones also contain proprioceptors. The term comes from the Latin
word "proprius" meaning "one's own." The sensations from one's own
body occur especially during movement; but they also occur while we
are standing still, for the muscles and joints constantly send information
to the brain to tell us about our position. Because there are so many muscles and joints in the body, the proprioceptive system is almost as large
as the tactile system.

Proprioception travels up the spinal cord to the brain stem and cerebellum, and some of it reaches the cerebral hemispheres. Most proprioceptive input is processed in regions of the brain that do not produce
conscious awareness, and so we rarely notice the sensations of muscles
and joints unless we deliberately pay attention to our movements. Even
if we try to be aware, we feel only a small fraction of all the proprioception
that is present during movement.

Proprioception helps us move. If there were less proprioception, our
body movements would be slower, more clumsy, and involve more effort.
If the proprioception from your hands were not sufficient to tell you
what your hands were doing, it would be very difficult to button clothes,
take something out of a pocket, screw a lid on a jar, or remember which
way to turn a water faucet. Without adequate proprioception from the
trunk and legs, you would have a very hard time getting in or out of an
automobile, walking down steep stairs, or playing a sport. You would
tend to rely upon visual information by looking closely at what your
body was doing. Children with poorly organized proprioception usually
have a lot of trouble doing anything when they cannot see it with their eyes.

The Vestibular Sense

On the other side of your outer ear is your *inner ear*. It contains a
very complex structure made of bone. This structure is called the *labyrinth* from the Greek word for a maze of winding passages. The labyrinth
contains both the auditory receptors and the two types of vestibular
receptors.

One type of receptor responds to the force of gravity. These receptors
consist of tiny calcium carbonate crystals attached to hair-like neurons.
Gravity pulls these crystals downward and the movement of hair-like
cells activates the nerve fibers of the vestibular nerve. This nerve carries
vestibular sensory input to the vestibular nuclei of the brain stem. Because gravity is always present on this planet, the gravity receptors send
a perpetual stream of vestibular messages throughout our entire life.
When the head bends to one side, moves up and down, or moves in any
direction that changes the pull of gravity upon the calcium carbonate
crystals, the vestibular input from the gravity receptors changes the

information in the vestibular system. The gravity receptors are also sensitive to bone vibration that shakes the crystals.

The second type of vestibular receptor lies in tiny closed tubes that are called the semicircular canals. These canals are filled with a fluid. There are three pairs of canals in each inner ear: one lying up and down, one left to right, and the third front to back. When the head moves rapidly in any direction, the fluid backs up in one or more pairs of the three semicircular canals in each ear. The pressure of the fluid backing up in the canals stimulates the receptors that lie inside the canals. The receptors then produce impulses that flow through the vestibular nerve to the vestibular nuclei. This sensory input changes whenever the head changes the speed or direction of its movement and so we call the input from the semicircular canals the sense of movement. Technically it should be called the sense of head "acceleration" or "deceleration."

The combination of input from the gravity receptors and the semicircular canals is very precise and tells us exactly where we are in relationship to gravity, whether we are moving or still, and how fast we are going and in what direction. It may be hard to realize that this information is actually being processed in your brain since the information is so basic that you cannot possibly imagine what it would be like not to process it.

The vestibular system is so sensitive that changes in position and movement have a very powerful effect on the brain, and this effect changes with even the most subtle change in position or movement. This effect begins very early in fetal life; the vestibular nuclei appear nine weeks after conception and begin to function by the tenth or eleventh week. By the fifth month in utero, the vestibular system is well developed and along with the tactile and visceral systems provides almost all of the sensory input to the fetal brain. Throughout most of pregnancy, the mother stimulates her fetus's vestibular system with the movements of her body.

Vestibular sensations are processed mostly in the vestibular nuclei and cerebellum. They are then sent both down the spinal cord and into the brain stem, where they serve a powerful integrating role. Some of them are sent from the brain stem to the cerebral hemispheres. The impulses going down the spinal cord interact with other sensory and motor impulses to help us with our posture, balance, and movement. The impulses going up to higher levels of the brain interact with tactile, proprioceptive, visual, and auditory impulses to give us our perception of space and our position and orientation within that space. Vestibular input seldom enters into our conscious awareness, except after we spin in circles and the input is so intense that we feel dizzy and see the world turn around us. Even when overstimulation of the vestibular system makes us "motion sick," we feel the problem in our bodies rather than in our inner ears.

The semicircular canals provide essentially the same information as a gyroscope in an airplane or space ship. If the gyroscope on a space ship were to break, there would be no way to know which direction the ship was traveling or when that direction changed, and the ship would very quickly get lost. Airplane pilots have tried to fly without a gyroscope by looking down at the earth, but ended up flying in circles or spirals. Visual information is useless unless one can relate what is seen to some physical reference. The semicircular canals provide the physical reference that gives proper meaning to our vision.

Visceral Input

There are receptors in the internal organs and in major blood vessels. Activity, blood flow, and blood chemical contents stimulate these receptors to provide the brain stem with the information needed to keep the body healthy. Visceral input helps to regulate blood pressure, digestion, breathing, and the other functions of the autonomic nervous system. Visceral input also tells the brain how much food and water is needed in the body. Other sensory systems, especially the tactile and vestibular systems, also influence the autonomic system. This is why spinning can upset our digestion and painful sensations can make us stop breathing. Although the visceral system is vital for survival and health, we shall not discuss it in detail in this book.

Sensations and the Whole Brain

When the activity of a sensory system becomes more organized, or various sensory systems become more integrated with one another, the nervous system functions in a more "holistic" manner. When an infant creeps across the room, or a child masters an obstacle course, his entire body works together as one balanced unit. The sensations from these full body adaptive responses generate a well-organized and balanced pattern of activity in the brain. When the whole body and all of the senses work together as a whole, adaptation and learning are easy for the brain.

The vestibular system is the unifying system. It forms the basic relationship of a person to gravity and the physical world. All other types of sensation are processed in reference to this basic vestibular information. The activity in the vestibular system provides a "framework" for the other aspects of our experience. Vestibular input seems to "prime" the entire nervous system to function effectively. When the vestibular system does not function in a consistent and accurate way, the interpretation of other sensations will be inconsistent and inaccurate, and the nervous system will have trouble "getting started."

The Evolution of the Nervous System

The brain is a difficult structure for scientists to study. It is encased in bone and not readily available for experimentation in human beings. Most of the research on the brain has been done on lower animals. While the human brain does differ in some structures and functions from that of lower animals, there are many basic similarities.

The human brain is the product of 500 million years of evolution in vertebrate animals. Vertebrates are animals with a backbone, such as fish, dogs, monkeys, and human beings. All vertebrates have a central nervous system—a spinal cord and a brain—in which sensations come together and responses originate. A jellyfish is an example of an invertebrate that has nerve cells but no central nervous system and little capacity to integrate sensations. The nerve cells are arranged in a *nerve net* throughout the entire body. When something touches a jellyfish, the sensations spread evenly through the entire network, which then causes the jellyfish to contract. The first vertebrates were primitive fish that had very simple central neural structures with the capacity to integrate only a few sensations. These primitive fish were the ancestors of modern fish, amphibians, reptiles, birds, and mammals.

The first structures and functions of the brain to develop have not changed very much. As the brain evolved, new structures and functions were added to these basic elements. The older parts of the brain continue to function today in much the same way as they did in our ancestors millions of years ago. Throughout evolution, each individual brain has operated according to certain timeless principles. Studying these principles helps us to understand the function of our brain today. Studying the evolution of the nervous system also tells us something about how the nervous system develops in our children.

The Adaptive Response

As the animal kingdom evolved, animals that could adapt successfully to nature survived and passed on their genes to their offspring. Animals that could not make adaptive responses to the demands of the environment did not survive to reproduce. In the animal world, adaptation is the ability to sense the body and the environment, interpret those sensations accurately, and make the proper motor response to obtain a meal, avoid being a meal for another animal, and deal with the harsh conditions of nature. Evolution included many periods in which animals found themselves in an environment where food was scarcer, enemies more common, nature even harsher. The animals that adapted and survived were able to do so because of good sensory-motor functions.

In early animals—up to about 100 million years ago—the brain consisted mostly of a brain stem and very rudimentary cerebellum and cerebral hemispheres. These animals—like fish and lizards today—were capable of little more than sensory and motor functions. For these animals to survive the demands of their environment, their sensory and motor functions had to become integrated into one unified and balanced process. The brain stem of man still handles about the same sensory and motor functions that it did in earlier animals.

Levels of Function

The earliest vertebrate nervous system was not much more than a spinal cord. Gradually new structures evolved onto the forward end of this spinal cord. The new "higher" structures did the same things as the older "lower" ones, but did them in more complex ways. A simple spinal cord can respond to touch with body movement, but in a diffuse, undifferentiated way. A brain stem can do an even better job of interpreting and responding to touch, but the cortex of the cerebral hemispheres can make the most precise interpretation and response, provided the brain stem is operating efficiently and sending on the sensory information well.

As each new structure evolved, its function remained somewhat dependent upon the older structures and functions. A business follows the same principle when it opens up a branch office; the new office depends upon the older established office. The cerebral cortex evolved out of the lower levels of the cerebral hemispheres, and so cortical processes depend upon lower cerebral hemisphere processes and also upon brain stem processes. The cortex cannot develop precise tactile, visual, and auditory perceptions unless the brain stem has developed its more fundamental tactile, visual, and auditory processes.

The Sensory Systems

The manner in which the sensory systems evolved influences the way in which they develop and function in man today. The evolution of the brain has been a 500-million-year process of improving the association among the sensory systems. In man, all of the sensory systems communicate with each other, and they function together inside of us much more than most of us realize. Schools make the mistake of trying to develop the child's visual and auditory systems independently of the other senses. Parents can partially rectify that mistake by allowing their children to get the tactile, vestibular, and proprioceptive experiences they want and need.

The evolution of touch. Even a one-celled animal such as an amoeba will respond to touch. Very primitive animals had three layers of body cells; the outer of these layers then evolved into both the vertebrate nervous system and the skin. Likewise, a few weeks after conception, the human embryo consists of three layers of cells, and the outer layer then develops into the nervous system and skin. Since both our nervous system and our skin come from the same origin, tactile stimuli have a primal role in neural organization. Touch sensations flow throughout the entire nervous system and influence every neural process to some extent. This helps to explain why the tactile system is involved in most disorders of the human brain.

For millions of years, the sense of touch was a major means of recognizing danger. Touch stimuli—except for those stimuli caused by the animal touching itself or a mother touching her infant—tended to prepare the animal to protect itself by fighting or running away. Touch also told the animal whether the surface under its feet was a safe place to stand. Touch sensations from the mouth helped the animal know what it was chewing and how to move the food about in its mouth. Many of these sensations were processed in the brain stem.

As higher animals evolved, they needed more detailed information from the skin to feel and manipulate things with their paws, to dig holes in the ground, and to climb trees. The demand for these abilities caused the evolution of nerve tracts that could carry more precise tactile information and areas in the cerebral hemispheres to process this information. As the tactile system evolved further, the increase in tactile perception skill enabled apes and early mankind to use primitive tools effectively.

Touch and emotion. In the course of evolution, the touch system became associated with emotional and social functions. Dr. Harry F. Harlow and his associates at the University of Wisconsin demonstrated this most clearly in their studies of infant monkeys. They took the newborn monkeys away from their mothers and raised them with artificial "mothers" made of wire or terry cloth. Harlow found that the monkeys hugged, clung to, and climbed on the terry cloth surface as if it were a real mother, and formed an emotional attachment to their artificial "mothers." Touching the terry cloth gave them the self-assurance to explore their environment and calmed them down when they were frightened. However, infants raised on "mothers" made of plain wire could not develop this emotional attachment and sense of security, even when the plain wire "mother" held a bottle of milk. This "mother" was uncomfortable to touch, and so it did not satisfy the infant's emotional needs. Harlow concluded that comfortable touch sensations are a critical factor in the infant's emotional attachment to his mother.

Harlow's conclusions seem to apply to all mammals, especially in the higher mammals who cannot care for themselves for a long time after birth. Nature has made human children dependent upon their mothers for a very long time, and during these years of dependence, the child needs a lot of touch sensations to develop the emotional security needed for later independence. Mothers have always known that hugging and caressing a baby will stop his crying. There was a time when people who knew very little about the brain and sensory integration told mothers to let the baby cry because picking him up would supposedly spoil him and make him cling to her later in life. However, it is more likely that holding and touching a baby will help him develop and organize the emotional processes of his brain so that he can function well as an independent adult.

Evolution of the vestibular and auditory systems. Every living thing—both plant and animal—must relate to the gravitational force of the earth. Gravity is the most constant and universal force in our lives. Throughout evolution, there has been a tremendous drive to master the earth's gravitational pull, and our upright posture is the culmination of that drive. We can even see this drive in some of the shellfish, which put grains of sand in a cavity in their heads so that they can feel the pull of gravity on the sand and know which way is up.

The need for rapid and efficient swimming caused the vestibular system to evolve in the first fish. This early vestibular system was so effective that it has remained essentially the same in amphibians, reptiles, birds, and mammals. Some of the connections to motor neurons have changed to enable each species to move in its own unique way, but the sensory functions of the fish's vestibular system were so ideal that nature retained them on the land, in the trees, and in the air. No other sensory system has a background of such consistency. Early fish had hair like receptor cells on the sides of their heads. These cells told the fish about ripples in the water that might mean danger. Then membranes evolved to enclose these receptor cells and form semicircular canals, gravity receptors, and auditory receptors. The movements of the fish made the fluid inside the sacs and canals stimulate the hair-like receptor cells and gave the fish a sense of its own movements through the water.

When the descendants of early fish adapted to life on the land, the auditory receptors evolved out of the primitive gravity receptors. Both vestibular and auditory senses were originally more a sense of tactile vibration. Harvey Sernat and Martin Netsky have traced the evolution of this vibratory sense. They point out that the first land animals lay with their heads touching the earth, and so the bones of their heads picked up ground vibrations. The capacity to "hear" ground vibrations still exists in man today. (You have probably seen movies in which cowboys or Indians listen to the ground to hear horses approaching.) As amphibians evolved, their heads rose away from the ground and a system evolved in the bones of their forelimbs that conducted ground vibrations up to their vestibular receptors. The ability to sense the movements of nearby animals was so important for survival that nature kept on finding new ways to deliver the information to the inner ears. In mammals and birds, the forelimbs could not conduct very well from the ground, so some of the vibratory receptors adapted to pick up vibrations in the air.

Once nature makes connections within the nervous system, these connections are rarely disconnected; instead, they are adpated for use in a different way. These old connections are still used in vertebrates, including man, but more recently evolved neural connections higher in the brain do most of the refined sensory processing. So the auditory system is still closely associated with the vestibular system, and both systems respond to vibration. Sensory integration therapists stimulate the vestibular system with movement or vibration to improve auditory and language processes. It is likely that such improvements occur through the very old neural connections between the vestibular and auditory senses.

The evolution of vision. From the very first vertebrates, the vestibular and visual systems were closely associated. In fish and amphibians, the visual system is organized to respond only to movement. Every fisherman knows that his bait must move, otherwise the fish will not notice it. Insects are usually moving, and so frogs never evolved the ability to see stationary objects well. Bulls are not attracted to the red color of the bullfighter's cape; they are interested only in its movement. Even cats and dogs are more likely to see something if it moves. The vestibular system must function efficiently to keep the eyes on a moving object, and to do so even when the animal itself is moving. Perceiving an object's movement is one of the oldest functions of the brain, and it is dependent upon brain stem sensory processing.

The ability to see a small nonmoving object evolved much later, when the cerebral hemispheres did, and is dependent upon good cerebral sensory processing. As with all other sensory-motor functions, the cerebral control will not develop well unless the brain stem control is there. Sometimes when a child is learning to read, he will move his finger underneath the line of print. He does this because it is easier to follow his moving finger than it is to focus on the stationary letters. This is a good example of how the child's inner drive directs him to stimulate his own brain in a way that helps it function. Vision has become our major means of relating to space, but the vestibular, proprioceptive, and touch systems must contribute to visual development and function.

Evolution of some adaptive responses. The adaptive responses of vertebrates helped to organize the sensations of gravity and the body. The
most basic and most consistent adaptive response has been to get into
the *prone position*. The prone position is the position in which locomotion
evolved, and it is the position from which animals stood up onto four legs
and then two legs. The prone position also protects the soft parts of the
body from danger. Turn an animal onto its back, and the neck-righting
reflex will make it struggle to return to prone. Since the vestibular receptors lie in three different planes of space, the position of the head determines which receptors are stimulated. All vertebrates swim, lie, walk, or
fly with their faces toward the ground, and this may be why the prone
position provides the vestibular input that is essential to sensory-motor
growth. Thus lying on the stomach is vital for normal sensory integrative
development.

After amphibians pulled themselves out of the water, they needed to
crawl on land. The reflex responses to gravity lifted first the head, and
then the upper trunk. Then the vestibular system helped to coordinate
the left and right limbs. The amphibians who were most successful at
crawling evolved into reptiles. Watch a lizard crawl rapidly over the
ground; notice the perfect organization of the limbs and trunk. Sarnat
and Netsky say that these movements are carried out almost entirely
through the lizard's vestibular system and vestibulospinal tracts.

As mammals evolved longer legs and more complex movements, their
muscles and joints sent more complex proprioceptive sensations to the
brain. Thus the proprioceptive system evolved after the tactile and vestibular systems and does not have as extensive connections to all the other sensory systems. The proprioceptive system is more specific in its functions.

The first mammals lived in the trees where sight and sound are very
important for finding food and evading other animals; this is when the
visual and auditory systems began their extensive development. Meanwhile the vestibular and proprioceptive systems continued to evolve for
climbing up and down and balancing on narrow limbs. Tree-living led
to many important adaptive responses and a great deal of sensory integration. Children love to climb for similar reasons.

Primitive reptiles, like the lizards of today, could not bring their paws
together. The first mammals, like modern squirrels, could bring the hands
together, but they could not use one hand on the other side of the body.
As monkeys evolved, they learned to cross the midline of the body, and
their improved reaching abilities enabled them better to meet the demands
of their environment. Pulling, pushing, picking up things, carrying them,
hitting, and hanging from tree limbs were useful for survival, and so the
genes that made these abilities possible were passed down from one gener-
ation to the next.

As the hand evolved and sent more precise sensations to the brain, apes
learned to use primitive tools. Vision became even more important for
survival because the nervous system has no built-in reflexes for using a

stick to dig a hole. However, the ape still had to feel the weight of the tool in his hand and keep his balance when he used it; and so the visual information from the stick was integrated with vestibular and proprioceptive signals from the body.

The sensations from the hands manipulating objects caused the cerebral cortex to evolve large areas for processing those sensations and directing more complex hand skills. After many years of tool-using, the sensations from the hand also enabled early man to develop the thumb that was opposite the fingers. The efficient action between the thumb and the other fingers made technology possible, and the increased sensory input and ability to make more complex adaptive responses caused further evolution of the sensory and motor cortex.

How the Nervous System Learns to Integrate Sensations

A child goes to school, but actually his nervous system has been learning since long before birth. At school he learns specific academic material; earlier in life his brain developed the *capacity* or ability to learn specific things, such as how to read or calculate. A large part of this capacity for learning is the ability to integrate sensory information.

The brain at birth knows how to integrate a few basic tactile, vestibular, and proprioceptive sensations, and so the newborn responds to stimuli as we have described in the preceding chapter. In this chapter, we have seen what the human nervous system is designed to do; now we shall try to draw a picture of what happens within each child's nervous system as it learns to function. Nobody knows exactly how learning takes place in the nervous system, but a few general things are known.

The Pathway of Neural Messages

Neural impulses must pass through two or more neurons to form a sensory experience, a motor response, or a thought. The more complex the function, the more neurons are involved in transmitting the message. Each neuron adds more elements to the person's experience and response. All human nervous systems function in certain characteristic ways, and so all of us perceive and respond in many similar ways.

How does each of us learn what various sensations mean and what to do about them? Why do particular messages get through in some of us, and not in others? Why don't we experience everything that stimulates our nervous system? What keeps us from over-responding?

Imagine yourself touching a hot stove with your finger. The heat activates tactile receptors in the skin of your finger, and these produce pain impulses that travel through sensory fibers in your hand, arm, and shoulder to your spinal cord. The sensory fibers end in the spinal cord and then release a chemical into the microscopic gaps known as synapses. The chemical carries the electrical energy across the synapses and into a group of motor neurons. These motor neurons carry the impulses back to muscles in the arm, hand, or fingers. These motor impulses cause the muscles to contract in a way that pulls your hand away from the stove.

The Synapse

The *synapses* are the places where neurons make electrochemical contact. They are bridges that carry impulses from one neuron to another. These "bridges" are made between the twig-like branches off the main fiber or off the cell body of the neuron. Neurons interact through synapses. The physical structure of most neurons does not change appreciably after early childhood, but the ability of a synapse to conduct neural impulses does change. Changes in the conductivity of synapses are the basis for learning, including the learning in school and at a job.

The reflex that pulls your hand away from pain involves a few synapses. Complex experiences involving motor coordination, emotion, and thought require the interaction of many neurons through countless synapses. In addition to stimulating the motor neurons, the pain impulses from the hot stove also cross synapses to enter neurons that travel up the spinal cord to the brain stem. From the brain stem, the impulses flow from one neuron to another, through various synapses, and produce effects in many parts of the brain. These effects include the awareness of pain, emotional reactions, voluntary behaviors (such as turning off the stove), thoughts, memories, and decisions (such as not to touch hot stoves anymore).

Every neural message divides and subdivides through thousands or millions of synapses in a fraction of a second. Every experience and activity in life involves an infinitely complex maze of neurons and synapses. To produce an appropriate perception or behavior, the impulses must stay on the right path. When sensory stimulation does not produce an appropriate perception or behavior, we know that somewhere in the nervous system neural messages are not crossing the synapses they should cross. They are getting lost in the maze.

Many impulses from different parts of the body and brain arrive at and effect the electrical and chemical energy of a single synapse. All of these impulses must blend in with each other in the synapses. For a message to cross a synapse and carry on to another part of the nervous system, the impulses must have great electrical strength, or they must be helped across by other impulses.

Facilitation and Inhibition

Some parts of the brain send out messages that help or *facilitate* other messages in crossing particular synapses. These messages are called *facilitatory* or *excitatory*. Other parts of the brain send out messages that hinder or *inhibit* the flow of messages across synapses. The combination of facilitatory and inhibitory messages produces *modulation*, which is the nervous system's process of self-organization. We modulate the sound coming out of a radio by turning the volume up or down. The nervous system modulates itself by increasing the energy of certain messages and reducing the energy of others.

For instance, messages from the vestibular nuclei facilitate motor messages throughout the spinal cord, and this helps maintain our muscle tone and body posture. Meanwhile the activity of the vestibular nuclei is inhibited by messages from the cerebellum, and this inhibition prevents vestibular activity from becoming excessive. Every sensory and motor process involves a complex arrangement of facilitatory forces to help the useful messages along and inhibitory forces to reduce the impulses that are not useful. Without sufficient inhibition, sensory impulses would spread like wildfire through the nervous system and nothing could ever be accomplished. The person would be overwhelmed. Facilitation and inhibition are both important parts of sensory integration. The ability to modulate sensation is one process the young child must learn in order to be able to deal with sensory stimulation later on in life.

The Growth of Neural Connections

A newborn infant has most of the neurons he will ever have, but a few more will grow in the first few years of life. However, at birth he has very few interconnections or synapses between his neurons. Clusters of interconnections grow between neurons during infancy. As your baby interacts with the world and the parts of his body, the sensory and motor impulses flowing among his neurons cause the fibers to grow branches and twigs reaching out toward other neurons.

Neurons must be stimulated to develop interconnections. A sensory system can develop only if it is exposed to the forces that activate its receptors. There must be light and something to see for the visual system to develop the interconnections needed for visual perception, sound for the auditory system to develop, and body movement for the vestibular and proprioceptive systems.

The growth of new interconnections produces new possibilities for neural communication. Each new interconnection adds new elements to the infant's sensory perceptions and motor abilities. The more neural interconnections a person has, the more capable he is of learning; and this is what intelligence really is.

Sensory stimulation and motor activity during the years of early childhood will "mold" the neurons and interconnections to form sensory and motor processes that will remain relatively stable for the rest of the person's life. Because the infant still has room in which to build new interconnections, he is very flexible in his perceptions and behaviors and learns rapidly and easily. The sensory and motor parts of the nervous system continue to be somewhat flexible during childhood. By age 10, the growth of sensory interconnections is complete or nearly complete in most parts of the brain. Older children and adults cannot develop new sensory interconnections as easily.

Learning in Older Children and Adults

The more a muscle is used, the stronger it becomes, up to a point. If it is not used, it becomes weak. Similarly, the more a synapse is used, the stronger and more useful it becomes. As with muscles, the use of a synapse makes that synapse easier to use; and the disuse of a synapse makes it harder to use that synapse. Every time a neural message crosses a synapse, something happens in the neurons and in the synapses to make it easier for other similar messages to cross that synapse in the future. Every time a sensory or motor process is repeated, less neural energy is needed to carry out that process the next time. This is what happens in thousands or millions of synapses at the same time when we practice a telephone number or a motor skill. The repeated use of the synapses gives us a memory of the number or makes the skill easier and then eventually automatic.

Learning How to Learn

The interaction of the sensory and motor systems through all their countless interconnections is what gives meaning to sensation and purposefulness to movement. The vestibular and tactile systems provide the most basic information. The proprioceptive system is next, and also conveys essential information. These three senses then give meaning to what is seen by associating the visual information with what is experienced in movement and in touch. Vision helps give meaning to what is heard, and hearing helps give meaning to what is seen. Finally, the meanings given to sensation help to form abstract and cognitive thoughts.

Without interaction with the physical environment, learning is very difficult. Most of our learning must occur first through the integration of our sensory systems. Later on, more intellectual and academic learning can take place in the cerebral cortex. Sensory-motor interaction provides the groundwork for later cognitive functions. It may look as though the child at play is not learning anything, but actually he is learning something very basic; he is learning how to learn.

Learning is a function of the whole nervous system. A child has difficulty learning to read if all of his sensory systems are not helping him to process the marks on the page. The more his sensory systems work together, the more he can learn and the easier it is for him. Learning begins with gravity and the body. Learning to sit upright, or shake a rattle, or walk down stairs, or hold a crayon develops the brain's capacity to learn more complex things. With the capacity developed on the sensory-motor level, the child is then better able to learn to add two numbers, or write a sentence, or relate to friends.

The Learning in Therapy

In sensory integration therapy we want the child to use as many synapses as he can comfortably. We especially want him to use the synapses in his brain stem in which many types of sensations come together. The child may look as though he is merely playing, but the work goes on within. It may not seem that he is improving in the area of his problem, but he is learning how to use his brain more effectively and easily. If he is young enough, he may be growing new interconnections, and his improvement will then be rapid. If he is older, therapy may help him learn how to facilitate certain messages and inhibit others, to direct information to the proper places in his brain and body, and to put all the messages together into useful perceptions and behaviors. His therapy is not to learn specific skills, such as how to read or write; he is learning to organize his brain so that it will work better. This will make him more able to learn reading and writing, and many other things as well.

REFERENCES

Harlow, Harry F. Love in infant monkeys. *Scientific American,* 1959, *200,* 68-74.

Harlow, Harry F. The nature of love. *American Psychologist,* 1958, *13,* 673-685.

Sarnat, Harvey B., & Netsky, Martin G. *Evolution of the nervous system.* New York: Oxford University Press, 1974.

II

SENSORY INTEGRATIVE DYSFUNCTION

CHAPTER 4

WHAT IS SENSORY INTEGRATIVE DYSFUNCTION?

Sensory integrative dysfunction is to the brain what indigestion is to the digestive tract. The word *dysfunction* is the same as "malfunction"; it means that the brain is not functioning in a natural, efficient manner. *Sensory* means that the inefficiency of the brain particularly affects the sensory systems. The brain is not processing or organizing the flow of sensory impulses in a manner that gives the individual good, precise information about himself or his world. When the brain is not processing sensory input well, it usually is also not directing behavior effectively. Without good sensory integration, learning is difficult and the individual often feels uncomfortable about himself, and cannot easily cope with ordinary demands and stress.

We can think of the brain as a large city and of neural impulses as the automobile traffic in that city. Good sensory processing enables all the impulses to flow easily and reach their destination quickly. Sensory integrative dysfunction is a sort of "traffic jam" in the brain. Some bits of sensory information get "tied up in traffic," and certain parts of the brain do not get the sensory information they need to do their jobs. Another term for this type of problem is *sensory integrative disorder.* If you have been in a rush-hour traffic jam, you know what disorder is.

Brain damage is one condition that usually leads to poor sensory processing. In most children with sensory integrative dysfunction, however, there is probably *not* actual damage to the structure of the brain. Indigestion does not mean that the stomach or intestines have been damaged; it simply means that these organs are not processing food properly. A traffic jam does not mean that the streets are damaged.

The term "dysfunction" is used to imply that there is some possibility that the problem may be reversed. *Minimal brain dysfunction* indicates that the problem is mild and might be at least partially corrected by therapy. There may be a way to reduce brain dysfunction just as there are ways to reduce indigestion and traffic jams.

Even though sensory integrative dysfunction is caused by irregular activity in the brain, most neurologists (physicians who specialize in the brain) will not find anything wrong in the child with sensory integrative dysfunction. Neurologists usually look for brain damage or something that is going to get worse, such as a tumor or a disease. Sensory integrative dysfunction is not something that will show up on his tests. It is not a disease and it is not going to get worse, although its effect on the child's life may become greater at times. Pediatric neurologists are beginning to recognize minimal brain dysfunction, and so they may be able to diagnose the child's problem.

Minimal brain dysfunction can cause many different problems; poor sensory integration is just one of these. It can, and often does, result in *aphasia* (difficulty in speaking and sometimes difficulty in understanding what others say), severe behavior problems, and other psychological problems. Some children with minimal brain dysfunction must have a carefully controlled diet because their brains cannot handle certain biochemicals the way that other brains do.

Minimal brain dysfunction is not the same as mental retardation, and neither is sensory integrative dysfunction. Many children with sensory integration problems have normal or above-average intelligence. If a child has poor sensory processing in many areas of his brain, he will probably have trouble dealing with ideas and generalizations and other intellectual matters, and so a very severe sensory processing problem can make a child mentally retarded. But most children with sensory integrative dysfunction do not have this severe a problem.

Children with sensory integrative dysfunction often develop in an uneven way. Since the problem is "minimal," only some parts of his nervous system function in a disordered or irregular way. Other parts will do their jobs normally, so the child will be up to age expectations in some functions and below in others. On the other hand, the mentally retarded child is apt to function pretty much the same in all areas. Sometimes his reasoning and ability to understand are poorer than his motor skills. The child with sensory integrative dysfunction is more likely to have greater problems with motor planning and lesser problems with reasoning and intellect.

Intelligence is the ability to interact with the physical environment or with thoughts and ideas. For this, the child needs a great deal of well-organized interaction among billions of neurons. Intelligence seems to correspond to the number of neurons in the brain and the number of connections between these neurons. Since most children with sensory integrative dysfunction have about as many neurons as normal children, their problem is caused by interconnections that work in an irregular way.

Let us illustrate these points with an analogy. Imagine a small business with a staff of four, and a similar business with a staff of eight. All things being equal, we might expect the eight-person business to do more work. Let us suppose that on one day, however, four of the people on the eight-person staff were absent, while all of the four-person staff was on the job. Although both businesses would have four people on duty, the full four-person staff would probably do better than the half eight-person staff.

Likewise, to produce full intelligence, a brain must have its full complement of neurons working together.

However, a sensory integrative dysfunction is a *malfunction*, not an *absence* of function. The eight-person staff might do very poor work if they did not talk to each other and coordinate their efforts. An eight-person staff of workers who do not talk to each other cannot do as well as a four-person staff that communicates freely. The child with sensory integrative dysfunction has a "full staff" of neurons, but these neurons are not talking to each other at certain times. They do not work together as a whole, and so some of what they do is useless or excessive.

Many people are beginning to realize that when a child has problems learning there may be something wrong with the way his brain is functioning. However, they do not understand that behavior problems are also rooted in the brain. Of course, many aspects of the environment are extremely important in determining how personality develops and expresses itself. Learning could not take place if there was nothing to learn about, and personality would not develop if the child did not interact with the circumstances of life. But the child's ability to interact is determined by the way his brain functions. Just as there are brains that cannot cope with algebra, there are also brains that cannot cope with stress, or changes in plans, or paying attention, or sharing with others, or even just sitting still.

However, not all problems in school are caused by sensory integrative dysfunction. If a person is blind, he does not get any visual information; but blindness is a deficit in sensory input rather than in sensory integration. If there is damage in the part of the brain that directs the muscles—as in cerebral palsy—the child cannot move well, but these are neuromuscular problems, not sensory integrative problems. If a child has an extremely stressful life, he may be very angry or withdrawn, but his problems are based on something other than poor sensory integration. Most children with sensory integrative dysfunction have normal eyesight and hearing, but these sensations do not have clear meaning for them. Most of these children have not suffered more hardship than the average person, but the disorder inside their brains has interfered with their emotional growth.

If the amount of irregularity is slight, the child's only apparent problem may be in learning—usually either learning to read or do math. Then school teachers and psychologists will say that he has a *learning disability*. Many learning problems are the result of poor sensory integration, and most children with learning disabilities have some degree of sensory integrative dysfunction.

Some people think that children with learning or behavior problems are merely slow developers. There are undoubtedly variations in growth rate that must be considered, but most professionals concerned with these problems have found that the child really does not ever completely grow out of his difficulties. Many children learn to compensate for their problem in some way, or accomplish things by working harder than other people do, or express their problem in some other way. It is very dangerous to think that a child will outgrow his problem, for this attitude prevents him from getting professional help at the age when it will do the most good.

The Symptoms and Their Possible Causes

What Causes the Problem?

We know less about what causes sensory integrative dysfunction than we know what to do about it. Some researchers think that certain children have a hereditary predisposition for certain types of minimal brain dysfunction. Many think that the increase in environmental toxins, such as air contaminants, destructive viruses, and other chemicals that we take into our bodies may contribute to the dysfunction. Hereditary and chemical factors may be combined in some children. The nervous system develops during fetal life, and the brain is very vulnerable at this time. Genetic factors in certain children may make one part of the brain more vulnerable than usual. In this highly vulnerable state, environmental toxins may interfere with sensory integrative development.

The brain is also vulnerable at birth and sometimes babies do not get enough oxygen at birth. Dr. W.F. Windle has conducted experiments in which he caused a similiar degree of oxygen deprivation in monkeys at birth. These monkeys showed signs of poor sensory processing, although later they seemed normal. When he dissected the brains of some of these monkeys, he found damage in the parts of the brain that process auditory and tactile stimuli. Windle's findings and other research have led some people to think that natural childbirth will reduce the frequency of minimal brain dysfunction.

Children who lead very deprived lives, having little contact with people or things, do not develop adequate sensory, motor, or intellectual functions. In institutions for homeless children the child is raised in a bare room with few opportunities for movement or play and little of the sensory stimulation that is usually provided by parents. This sensory deprivation results in poor development. Dr. Lawrence Casler gave a few institutionalized children extra tactile stimulation through gentle pressure on the surface of the skin and found it helped those children to develop better than those who did not receive the extra touching.

In the preceding chapter we discussed Harlow's experiments with infant monkeys that had been deprived of maternal sensory stimulation. The monkeys raised on an artificial "mother" made of wire could not get the comfortable touch sensations needed for their emotional growth. These monkeys grew up to have severe disorders and showed many of the stimulus-seeking behaviors common in institutionalized children.

Dr. Seymour Levine found that rats that were not touched and handled during infancy failed to develop the hormonal responses that maintain organized brain activity during stress. These rats were afraid to explore a new environment and overreacted to unfamiliar situations. As with Harlow's monkeys, the problem seemed to be due to the lack of tactile stimulation during the period when the brain needs these sensations to develop properly. However, the rats were never picked up or moved, and so the deprivation of vestibular stimulation was probably just as damaging. Drs. W.A. Mason and G. Berkson did experiments similar to Harlow's, except that they compared monkeys raised with an artificial cloth-covered "mother" that swung and rocked with monkeys that had similar "mothers" that were stationary. The infants with stationary "mothers" developed the abnormal behavior patterns, while the infants whose "mothers" had rocked and swung did not develop these abnormalities.

Drs. W.R. Thompson and Ronald Melzack at McGill University raised some Scottish terriers in cages—one to a cage—so that the dogs could not see outside the cage. When these dogs were seven to 10 months old the researchers compared them with litter mates that were raised normally. Both groups of dogs were shown strange objects; the normal dogs simply ran away, but the deprived dogs jumped about excitedly and even bumped into the object in their confusion. In other situations, they behaved wildly and aimlessly. They had trouble adapting to changes and engaging in purposeful activity. They couldn't remember where their food was, find their way through mazes, or socialize well. Even though these dogs were born with potentially normal brains, the deprivation of sensory stimulation and adaptive responses gave them little chance to develop.

Deprivation of sensory stimulation disorganizes the brain even in normal, healthy adults. Scientists noticed temporary behavior and personality problems in jet pilots after long flights in which they could not move from their seats and in persons stranded in cabins during Arctic winters. If you have had the experience of being confined to a hospital bed for a long time, or have taken long automobile trips in which you could not move about, you may remember the discomfort and irritability that comes from deprivation of vestibular and proprioceptive stimulation and adaptive responses to those sensations.

Some scientists designed *sensory deprivation chambers* to see what would happen if all the senses were *not* stimulated in a normal adult. It is literally impossible to deprive a living nervous system of sensation itself, but it is possible to deprive a person of *sensations that change.* This is done by removing all sensations except for monotonous sensations that activate the brain only slightly. After a short while, the brain stops processing monotonous sensations—such as the tick of a clock—and so these sensations provide no nourishment for the brain.

Some of the sensory deprivation chambers consisted of tepid water, which after a short time deprived the skin of stimulating sensations. In others, the person was in a head-to-toe suit that eliminated tactile stimulation and body movement. He was blindfolded or given a continuous field of white light. His ears were plugged or monotonous "white noise" was played into them. After several hours of this, the person's mental processes began to disorganize. He experienced abnormal anxieties, and visual and auditory hallucinations. Normal perceptual processes disintegrate when the brain is deprived of sensory nourishment. These problems often continued for some time after the person left the deprivation chamber.

The above experiments demonstrated what overt sensory deprivation does to sensory processes. However, overt sensory deprivation is usually *not* the cause of sensory integrative dysfunction in this country. Most of the children with these minor irregularities in brain function have had normal sensory experiences. Their parents or guardians did a good enough job of raising them to allow for normal brain development; and if there had not been a neurologic disorder, the child would have developed like other children. The parents did not deliberately or accidentally produce the dysfunction.

Although most of the children with sensory integrative dysfunction did not suffer the overt sensory deprivation that occurs in institutions or in experiments such as Harlow's, their problems may be the result of an "internal sensory deprivation." The sensory stimulation may have been present in the child's environment, but somehow, in this particular child, these sensations did not nourish every part of the brain that needed them. The sensations entered his brain, but some of them never reached the neurons and synapses they should have reached. Such internal sensory deprivation prevents the brain from developing the functions that depend on full sensory processing.

Parents usually do not realize that their child's learning and behavior problems are the results of neurologic disorders that the child cannot control; they think that he is doing things on purpose, and so they react in ways that make his life even more difficult than it is already. The damage caused by poor judgment in raising the child is usually after the fact. The problem was there in the brain before the parents did anything wrong. Instead of feeling guilty, do something to help the child organize his nervous system, or at least help him to feel better about himself.

The Symptoms

Sensory integrative dysfunction would be much easier to recognize and treat if the problem were the same in each child. Sensory integrative therapists have a somewhat bewildering diagnostic job since every child they see has his own set of symptoms. Some of these symptoms occur together often enough to consider them in *syndromes*, but most children do not fit exactly into these categories.

In the next four chapters we shall discuss these symptoms in detail and explain their significance. The following is a brief overview of these symptoms in common lay terms.

Hyperactivity and distractibility. Because it is so obvious and disruptive, hyperactivity or hyperkinesis is often the first sign of sensory integrative dysfunction that parents notice, and it is often a major complaint. The child is moving about almost all the time. He usually runs instead of walking, and much of his activity is not purposeful. Sitting still and concentrating are almost impossible. *Distractibility* is a major problem at school. Since the child cannot "shut out" the noises and lights and confusion of many people doing different things, he can never work up to his potential.

As a young child, he is "all over the place." When older, he may suppress some of the running, but the same excess neural activity may prevent him from keeping his room in order or getting his homework done or getting off to school with everything he needs. Parents often remark: "If he remembers his sweater, he forgets his lunch. If he remembers his lunch, he forgets his books."; "She just can't get her act together." If a brain cannot organize sensory input and motor activity, then it also cannot organize a closet full of clothes or a satchel of books, papers, and pencils.

Behavior problems. The child with minimal brain dysfunction is apt to give his parents more trouble than other children. He is less happy— things are just not right within him. He is fussy and cannot enjoy being with his family or playing with other children. Losing a game is very threatening to his incomplete self-concept, and so he ruins the game. Sharing his toys or his food may be difficult. He is forever trying to make himself feel successful and important, and so he cannot think about the needs of other people. Because his brain responds differently, he reacts differently to circumstances. He is overly sensitive and his feelings are often hurt. He cannot cope with everyday stress, or new and unfamiliar situations.

Because others do not like his behavior, they dislike him and make trouble for him. Children can be very mean to each other, and parents can also lose control. A vicious circle of negative self-concept, unpleasant behavior, and negative reactions by others keeps the child in misery. Not only must the dysfunctional child put up with his handicap, but he must also put up with other people who dislike and reject his actions. He may tend to play either with younger children who cannot challenge him or with older children who understand and accept him, or he may associate only with adults.

Speech development. Because speech and language depend upon many sensory integrative processes, they are apt to develop slowly whenever there is irregularity in any aspect of sensory processing. Society places great emphasis on speech for interpersonal communication, and so parents often notice poorly developed speech and articulation before they notice other more subtle symptoms.

Muscle tone and coordination. The sensations from the vestibular and proprioceptive systems provide the muscle tone that keeps the body upright and energetic. The child with sensory integrative dysfunction often has low muscle tone, which makes him seem weak. He has to use a lot of effort just to hold his head and body up against the pull of gravity, and so he gets tired very quickly. Because he lacks adequate muscle tone in his neck, he will have to rest his head on his hand or arm while sitting at a desk. He may lean against a wall or pole, because standing alone is too much work.

When the vestibular, proprioceptive, and tactile systems are not working well, the child is apt to have poor motor coordination. He may lose his balance and stumble easily. He may drop his pencil more often than other children. Some children even fall out of their chairs because they cannot feel exactly where they are on the seat. Clumsy movements are often caused by poor processing of body and gravity sensations, although they may also be caused by other neurological conditions. Immature play is a very common early sign of sensory integrative dysfunction. The child who cannot build with blocks, manipulate toys, or put puzzles together probably has a sensory integrative problem.

Learning at school. If the problem in the brain is minor, everything may seem all right until the child encounters school work. Reading, writing, and arithmetic require a great deal of sensory integration and make very complex demands upon the brain. A sensory integrative problem may interfere directly with the learning process in the brain, or it may cause poor behavior that interferes with school work even though the child has a normal capacity for learning. If school work becomes too discouraging, the child will cut classes and eventually drop out of school.

Learning to read and write may be major problems. The child must remember whether the *m* goes up or down and whether the *p* goes to the left or the right. This knowledge comes from some sort of visual or muscular memory that comes automatically for most people. But if the activity in the brain is disorganized, the child cannot "find" these memories when he needs them. Asking the kindergarten child to learn reading before his brain is ready for this task will not only be unproductive, but also take the child away from sensory-motor activities that his brain needs now in order to learn reading at a later age. Children with certain types of sensory integrative dysfunction always find writing difficult. Some children find it especially hard to hear words and then write them down; they cannot integrate the sound sensations with the sensations from their hands and fingers. The child may say, "I know what you want, but I can't write it down."

In general, the child with sensory integrative dysfunction has trouble dealing with the space around him. He may often bump into people or things because he has no way to judge where things are in space and where his own body is in space. He is literally "lost in space." In school, this problem may make it difficult to copy words from the blackboard onto paper. First the child has trouble with the space between himself and the blackboard, and then he has more trouble spacing the letters as he writes them on his paper. His letters may vary in size or be arranged crookedly.

Teen-age problems. By the time the child with a sensory integrative problem reaches his teens, he may have learned how to deal with academics well enough to limp along; if not, he may drop out of school. Many juvenile delinquents were originally children with sensory integrative disorders that interfered with their success in school. If the disorder is less severe, it may show up in smaller problems; for instance, occasionally turning to the wrong side, or difficulty remembering a sequence of numbers such as a telephone number, or trouble counting out change. Teenagers with poor sensory integration will probably avoid dancing and may even have trouble clapping out a simple rhythm to music. It is easy to see how such problems could make a teen-ager miserable.

One of the most common complaints of parents with teen-agers having sensory integrative dysfunction is lack of organization. The brain that has trouble organizing sensations has trouble organizing other things as well. Focusing on a task, such as cleaning up a room or writing a book report, is very difficult. For the teen-ager with poor sensory integration, it is especially difficult to plan a series of tasks, just as during childhood it was hard to understand a series of letters or numbers. He does not know what to do first or how long each action will take. If he is interrupted, he forgets what he was doing. There are some days when it is impossible to concentrate on and finish anything.

The Sensory Integrative Dysfunction Itself

The symptoms discussed above are not the real problem; they are the end products of inefficient and irregular sensory processing in the brain. To help us see how sensory integrative dysfunction underlies these symptoms, we have drawn a diagram (Figure 2) to show how different types of sensory information come together to form the functions a child needs to be successful and happy in life. You will probably find it helpful to refer back to this diagram as you read later chapters in this book.

On the far right of the diagram, we see the things that a person needs in order to relate to family and friends, do academic work, and work at a job as an adult. With the capacity for learning, a healthy personality and purposefulness, a person can "make it" in life. However, these things do not just appear in a human being; they are the culmination of many years of development and integration in the brain. What does a child need to get to that stage? What has gone awry in children who cannot get there?

To the far left of the diagram, we see the major sensory systems. The first requirement is adequate stimulation of these senses and a good flow of impulses from the receptors to the brain, and the child with sensory integrative dysfunction generally meets this requirement. His failure is in the integration of these sensory impulses.

We have used brackets to represent four "levels" of the sensory integrative process. The fault of this diagram is that it does not show the fluidity of the process in life. The functions listed on the diagram do not develop in great leaps followed by plateaus. Everything develops together, but some functions lead up to others.

The meaning of the brackets is exactly what they look like: many things coming together into one. The bracket after "tactile" indicates that touch sensations from every bit of skin come together for several types of use: one, to help the child suck and eat; another, to form a "mother-infant bond." The bracket that brings "vestibular" and "proprioceptive" together in the child leads to well-organized eye movements, posture, physical balance, muscle tone, and "gravitational security."

The next level is reached when the three basic senses—tactile, vestibular, and proprioceptive—are integrated into a body percept, coordination of the two sides of the body, motor planning, attention span, activity level, and emotional stability. The bracket indicates that visual and auditory sensations do *not* make a significant contribution to the development of these functions. The child sees and hears, but the organization of his nervous system depends upon the more basic sensations.

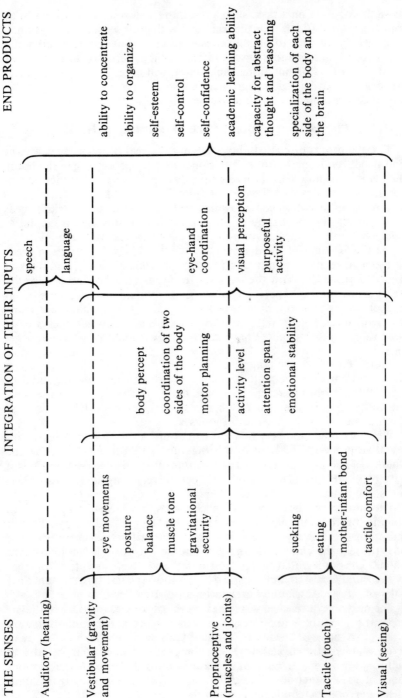

Figure 2. The Senses, Integration of Their Inputs, and Their End Products

At the third level of sensory integration, auditory and visual sensations enter the process. Auditory and more vestibular sensations come together with the body percept and related functions to enable the child to speak and understand language. Visual sensations are integrated with the three basic senses to give the child accurate, detailed visual perception and eye-hand coordination. As this third level is reached, the child does things that are more purposeful—for instance, eating with a spoon or fork, drawing, or putting things together and taking them apart.

At the fourth level, everything comes together to form the functions of a whole brain. The things in this level are end products of every sensory process that took place in the first three levels. The ability to organize and concentrate is part of academic learning capacity. Self-esteem, self-control, and self-confidence come from feeling the body as a competent sensory-motor being, and from good neurological integration. Once the two sides of the body can work together in purposeful activity, there is a natural specialization of the two sides of the body and brain.

None of these functions develops at just one age. The child works at each level of sensory integration throughout childhood. At two months, his nervous system is working a great deal at the primary level of integration, a bit less at the secondary level, and not so much at the third. At one year, the primary and secondary levels are most important, and the third level is becoming more important. At age three, he is still working on the primary, secondary, and third levels, and the fourth has begun. At age six, the primary level should be complete, the secondary level almost complete, the third level still active, and the fourth becoming important. The child learns the same things over and over again, first in crawling, then in walking, then in riding a bicycle.

The Primary Level of Integration

Touching and being touched have a very important influence on the infant and on the rest of his life. Touch sensations help him to suck, and then later to chew and swallow food. Infants with poorly functioning touch systems may have trouble sucking, and later on may not like to eat solid food because of its texture.

An infant needs to have bodily contact with his mother or a caretaker, and his brain must interpret the sensations from that contact correctly in order for him to form his first emotional attachment. Harlow showed that this emotional attachment is primarily tactile in nature. Some people have called this tactile-emotional attachment the "mother-infant bond." Bonding gives the infant his first feelings of himself as a physical body. The skin is the boundary of the self, and thus tactile processing is a primary source of security for the infant. Harlow demonstrated this by putting his monkeys in rooms with strange objects. The infants that had been reared on a terry cloth "mother" explored the room and its objects freely, although when their "mother" was in the room they occasionally glanced toward her for reassurance. The infants that had been reared on an uncomfortable wire "mother" could not tolerate being in an unfamiliar environment.

Even if a mother hugs and caresses her baby, the stimulus will not satisfy the infant's needs if poor sensory integration interferes with the processing of touch sensations. If this first attachment is incomplete, it will be harder to form emotional attachments later in life. Without tactile security from the mother-infant bond, the individual grows up to be less secure emotionally. Children with tactile disorders very often have trouble being affectionate, although they need affection even more than the normal child. They overreact to the everyday demands of life. They may have trouble doing things on their own.

Integration of vestibular and proprioceptive inputs gives the child control over his eye movements. Without the guidance of these sensations, it is difficult for the child to focus on an object or follow it as it moves. Later on it may be difficult to move the eyes along a line of print. Reading may be so exhausting that it simply isn't worth the effort.

If vestibular and proprioceptive systems are poorly integrated, the child may be slow to develop postural reactions, such as rolling over or getting into a creeping position, and so he will not have a good "foundation" for standing and walking. He may never learn to make postural adjustments that occur automatically in most people, and so his movements may seem stiff and irregular. His balance may be poor and his muscle tone low. Although he may compensate for these problems later on in life, they will still slow him down somewhat and cause fatigue.

Tactile sensations are a primal source of comfort and security. Another primal source of security is gravity. Gravitational security is the trust that one is firmly connected to the earth and will always have a safe place to be. This trust comes from sensing the gravitational pull of the earth and organizing those sensations so that one is "on friendly terms" with gravity. If the sensory information from the inner ears and from the muscles and joints is not integrated properly, the child will have a hard time knowing where he is in space and how he is moving. He may be in constant fear of falling or being tossed in the air. Because his relationship to gravity is insecure, he is insecure as a whole person. If he also lacks the emotional security that comes from good tactile processing, his emotional growth is severely threatened. None of us can imagine the terror the child feels when he cannot modulate ordinary tactile and vestibular sensations.

The Second Level of Sensory Integration

Tactile, vestibular, and proprioceptive functions are the building blocks for emotional stability. If these three basic sensory systems are not functioning adequately, the child will probably react poorly to his environment. Some children become withdrawn and quiet and try very hard to please others. Others are hyperactive and respond to every auditory and visual stimulus that comes their way. But auditory and visual sensations are not the problem here; the child is hyperactive because his basic sensory processes do not keep him stable. Although he is very active, he does not pay attention to what he is doing, and so he rarely accomplishes anything. He cannot get his brain to focus on anything. He is a very difficult child to have at home or in a classroom.

This is the child who has a poorly organized body percept. A *body percept* consists of body "maps" that are stored in the brain. These maps contain information about every part of the body, the relationships among all the parts, and all the movements each part can make. The body percept is stored in the brain as the sensations from the skin, muscles, joints, and gravity and movement receptors are organized and sorted during the child's daily activities. A well-organized body percept enables a person to *feel* what his body is doing without looking at it or touching it with his fingers. Visual information is not an important part of the body percept. If a child relies too much on looking at things, he probably has a poor body percept.

If his body percept does not contain a lot of good, clear information about the relationships between the left and right sides of the body, the child will have trouble doing things that require both hands or both feet together. Playing a toy drum or dancing are especially hard. Poor coordination of the two sides of the body is often seen in children with vestibular disorders.

If the brain does not have accurate "maps" of the body, then it cannot "navigate" or plan body movements. Most adults can use a fork or put on a shirt automatically, but a young child must "motor plan" these actions. Motor planning is the sensory process that enables us to adapt to an unfamiliar task and then learn how to do that task automatically. The key to motor planning is a body percept with accurate tactile, proprioceptive, and vestibular information. If a child does not have good "maps" of his body, he cannot direct unfamiliar movements and he takes a long time to learn them. Meanwhile his poorly organized nervous system will "drive" him into a lot of poorly planned movements. He may have trouble playing with toys, and often break them. He does not want to break his toys, but he can't feel how they can be manipulated, and so he pushes or pulls too hard.

The organization of a child's brain can be seen in his attention span and activity level. If sensations are out of control, the child will not be able to focus his attention or his activity. Auditory or visual stimuli may distract or overexcite a child, and usually do so when sensations from the body and from gravity are not well organized.

The Third Level of Sensory Integration

Sensory integration is a continuously flowing process, and each level of integration makes the next level possible. Before the child can understand words, he must be able to pay attention to the speaker. Before he can form words, he must have good sensory information from his mouth. The auditory-language center of the brain also needs sensations from the vestibular system. Thus Figure 2 shows that speech and language depend upon the integration of auditory sensations with the vestibular system.

As we noted in the preceding chapter, the auditory and vestibular systems are intimately related. Listening to people using language is, of course, essential for language comprehension and speech development, but the vestibular system must help the brain process what is heard.

Children with certain types of vestibular disorders are slowed down in their speech development, although once speech comes, it is often normal.

Articulation of words requires all three of the basic sensory systems. Even a simple one-syllable word like "toy" or "cat" requires very precise placement of the tongue and lips. Many children with sensory integrative dysfunction cannot feel exactly where their tongues are and how their lips are touching, and so their words are hard to understand.

Like speech and language, visual perception is an end product of the earlier sensory integration. Visual perception is the meaning you get from what you see. The simplest visual perception is the recognition of what something is. A more advanced perception is seeing an object in relationship to other objects and the background. Visual space perception tells us many things about the world: Is the cup upside-down or right side up? Will the peg go through the hole in the block? Will this piece of the puzzle fit into that space? How do I put this card into the envelope so that the address shows through the window of the envelope?

It is obvious that we need to see to know the answers to these questions, but the ability to see is not enough. It takes a lot of experience in touching objects, holding and moving them and feeling their weight through our muscles and joints, and interacting with the forces of gravity and momentum to develop visual perception. Sensations from the vestibular system are particularly important in this development, and so children with vestibular disorders will have some problems seeing what things mean. If vestibular function is very poor, the child will have poor depth perception and have trouble on stairs and heights. If the tactile and proprioceptive systems are also not working well, activities like pouring milk from a pitcher or setting a table will be difficult.

The child's activities become much more purposeful at this level of integration. He can do things that begin, continue, and end, and he can follow the process through to the purpose he wants. Reaching for a rattle, creeping across the room to play with something, picking up a toy, putting a peg into a hole, and climbing are all purposeful activities. The normal child can be purposeful in his actions because his basic sensory processes work in a stable, consistent, and reliable way. The child with sensory integrative dysfunction can't follow something through to the end because there are too many things that confuse, distract, overexcite, or upset him.

A lot of purposeful activity is done with eyes directing the hands. Vestibular and proprioceptive sensations direct many of our hand movements, but for tasks that are either very precise or unfamiliar, we need to look at what we are doing. Good eye-hand coordination means that the hands and fingers go exactly to the places where the eyes tell the brain that they should go. It is not enough merely to integrate the information from the eyes with the messages to the hands; the brain also needs relevant information from gravity and movement receptors and the muscles, joints, and skin of the *entire* body. The brain is designed to work as a whole and that is the only way it can work well. If the information from any sense is disorderly, the end product suffers. Thus children with vestibular, tactile, or proprioceptive disorders often have trouble with eye-hand coordination. They cannot tell where or how to draw lines or color between the lines. Later on they cannot do a neat job with a hand tool.

The Fourth Level of Sensory Integration

If the nervous system has worked well as a whole, different parts of the brain develop greater efficiency in processing certain types of sensory input and organizing certain adaptive responses. This specialization of function is important for optimal development of the brain and all of its functions. The most obvious form of specialization is the use of the right hand for fine motor skills—unless the person is genetically left-handed. Meanwhile the left hand—in right-handed persons—is usually better at interpreting tactile input and distinguishing what is in the hand. Something of a similar nature occurs in the brain to make one cerebral hemisphere—usually the left—more proficient at understanding and using language, while the other side is better at perceiving spatial relationships.

Before the different parts of the brain can specialize, they must work together and communicate with each other. If the two sides of the brain cannot work together and communicate, they both tend to develop similar functions. The child whose sensory integrative dysfunction has led to poor specialization will tend to use both hands or either hand for fine motor work, but he will not use either hand as well as a child with normal specialization. The poor communication between the two sides of his brain will also prevent the two sides of his body from working well together. The person often does not get a good, clear feeling of which is right and which is left. He might use a mental device, such as remembering that the left hand is the one with the ring on it.

The person with a well-developed body percept does not need such mental devices, because he gets the information from the sensory "maps" stored in his brain. As an infant and child, he coordinated his hands countless times during play. He has learned the difference between left and right in a sensory-motor manner, and that physical knowledge is the basis for good communication between the two sides of the brain.

When there is normal specialization of brain functions, one eye leads when the two eyes work together in binocular or depth vision, and that eye is also usually used for sighting, such as when we look down the eyepiece of a camera or microscope.

The importance of specialization has given professionals concern for many years, and some have tried to force the brain to specialize, thinking that this would help the child in learning and language. But this has not worked well. Specialization is an end product of all the earlier developmental steps. Forcing a child to develop an end-product function is never as good as helping him to mature in each of the steps that eventually lead to the end product. Specialization will occur naturally only after the child has filled in the gaps in his sensory-motor development.

The four levels of sensory integration should be well developed by the time the child enters school, for this is when he needs the end products of sensory integration. The ability to organize and concentrate is important since the child must now deal with many more people and things. The brain that cannot organize sensations will also not be able to organize letters or numbers. Self-esteem, self-control, and self-confidence are very important in relating to other people, but these feelings about one's self do not come without a lot of sensory and other neural integration beforehand.

If there are gaps and irregularities in any of the integrative steps before the child goes to school, there will be gaps and irregularities in his school work and in his life as a whole. Sometimes the inadequacies will be slight, sometimes large; sometimes they will be expressed in one way, sometimes in another. Sometimes adults will think that the schools are not doing a good job of teaching. Often—all too often—they will see these inadequacies as behavior problems and punish the child for them. Most people see only the end products of poor sensory integration; that the child is hostile or that he is shy, that his activity is excessive or aimless, that he forgets things or bumps into them, that he cannot read, write, or add two numbers. They tend to think that he is "goofing off" or trying to make trouble or not "using his head." However, when we try to stop bad behavior or force the child to concentrate, we only confuse him further. Most children do not want to misbehave, but if we continue to treat the child who has sensory integrative dysfunction as if he were a "bad child," he may then intentionally misbehave.

Splinter Skills

Although a child may not have developed the sensory integrative foundation for a function, society still demands that he perform that function. Therefore as the child with sensory integrative dysfunction grows older, he learns "splinter skills" that compensate for his poor sensory processing. An example of a splinter skill is the ability to play a particular piece on the piano without having the generalized ability to play the piano. If a child cannot learn to tie his shoes through the natural interaction of sensory information in his brain, he will have to learn to tie the knot as a splinter skill. Natural learning through sensory integration is easier, and each learning experience helps the brain learn many other things. Learning a splinter skill takes a lot of effort and concentration and does not help the child in other areas of his life. However, many splinter skills are worth having for their own sake.

If a child with sensory integrative dysfunction is bright, he will learn many splinter skills and appear to have normal physical, mental, and social functions, but life and just "being" will not be the same as they are for those with adequate sensory integration. With understanding and supportive parents, the child will often lead a gratifying life and carry his share of society's responsibilities. However, if the stresses of life are too much for his brain's coping abilities, he may then become one of life's "drop-outs."

REFERENCES

Casler, Lawrence. The effects of extra tactile stimulation on a group of institutionalized infants. *Genetic Psychology Monographs,* 1965, *71,* 137-175.

Levine, Seymour. Stimulation in infancy. *Scientific American,* May, 1960.

Mason, William A., & Berkson, Gershon. Effects of maternal mobility on the development of rocking and other behaviors in rhesus monkeys: A study with artificial mothers. *Developmental Psychobiology,* 1975, *8,* 197-211.

Serafetinides, E.A., Shurley, J.T., Brooks, R., & Gideon, W.P. Electrophysiological changes in humans during sensory isolation. *Aerospace Medicine,* 1971, *42,* 840-842.

Thompson, William R., & Melzack, Ronald. Early environment. *Scientific American,* 1956, *194,* 38-42.

Windle, William F. Brain damage by asphyxia at birth. *Scientific American,* 1969, *221,* 76-84.

CHAPTER 5

DISORDERS INVOLVING THE VESTIBULAR SYSTEM

Imagine four young children walking the narrow curb of a sidewalk. The first child walks gracefully along the curb two or three times and enjoys doing so. The second child has a hard time keeping his balance and repeatedly steps off the curb. The third child walks along without particular grace; he looks at his mother and makes some sounds but cannot speak well. The fourth child is afraid of falling, but his mother urges him to try. Holding her hand tightly, he walks the curb without falling.

The second, third, and fourth children are not adequately processing sensory input within their vestibular systems. Very few people realize that vestibular disorders do exist and cause problems in many children, and so this explanation is not widely accepted by physicians, educators, or other professionals. We know that some people have disorders in their auditory or visual systems and have poor perception of things seen or heard. It is just as likely that a disorder may occur in the vestibular system.

It is obvious that disorder in the vestibular system might make a person lose his balance or feel dizzy. This is what happens when a problem develops in the vestibular system after it has grown to maturity, such as when an adult gets a disease that damages the inner ears. However, if the problem begins in utero, or during birth, or infancy, the picture is different.

The first child in our example has normal sensory integration. The second child, who has trouble keeping his balance, looks and acts healthy but he has great difficulty in reading. The third child does not speak as well as other children his age, and he may be clumsy at some activities. The fourth child, who feels very anxious about falling, reads adequately, but he will probably develop emotional or behavior problems.

Although some of these problems seem to have little to do with poor balance or dizziness, they are to some extent caused by inadequate sensory processing in the vestibular system. How can the vestibular system be involved in so many important functions? The answer to that question is that the vestibular system has many interconnections with

69

almost every other part of the brain. These connections were discussed in Chapter 3. We shall review them in the next section.

Organization of the Vestibular System

When the vestibular system works normally, the pull of gravity generates a constant sensory flow from early fetal life until death. All other sensory inputs are superimposed upon that input from the gravity receptors. Since the effect of gravity upon our brains is constant throughout life, we take it for granted. However, the sensations from gravity flowing through our nervous system help to form a basic reference for all other sensory experiences.

Every change in head position stimulates some of the vestibular receptors. When we bend our head to the side or hold it upside-down, gravity pulls the calcium carbonate crystals away from their normal position in the head, and this changes the flow of impulses in the vestibular nerve. Jumping up and down makes the crystals go up and down to stimulate another pattern of vestibular input. Running and swinging move them in another direction, and also cause the fluid in some of the semicircular canals to back up into the sensitive receptors. Spinning activates one of the canals in each ear. Touching something that vibrates causes the bones to vibrate, and this stimulates the gravity receptors. Such activities provide a great deal of vestibular input. Standing, walking, and riding in a moving vehicle move the head in more subtle ways and provide milder streams of vestibular input. The vestibular receptors are the most sensitive of all sense organs. Nature would have made a sensory system this sensitive only if the information was extremely important for adaptation.

 The vestibular nuclei are the "business centers" that process vestibular input along with information from the muscles, joints, skin, and visual and auditory receptors. In addition, they organize impulses from many other parts of the brain, including the rest of the brain stem, the cerebellum, and many parts of the cerebral cortex. These nuclei send out impulses to all the areas that send impulses in to them. They begin to operate about nine weeks after conception and produce adaptive responses to vestibular input from movements of mother's body. The brain senses and responds to vestibular input long before we process visual and auditory inputs, and this vestibular activity provides some of the building blocks for the later development of seeing and hearing. The structure and function of the vestibular nuclei are far more complex than the most advanced computer. In a particular brain, some of these functions work normally, while others do not.

Modulation

One of the most important things that happens in the brain is the modulation of vestibular activity. *Modulation* is the process of increasing or reducing a neural activity to keep that activity in harmony with all the other functions of the nervous system. All of the functions of the brain must be in harmony with each other to produce the most effective adaptive response.

To understand the process of modulation, you can think of listening to a radio. When vestibular activity is too "loud" and disturbs the rest of the nervous system, certain parts of the brain inhibit or "turn off" some of that activity. When the "volume" of vestibular activity is too low, other parts facilitate or excite that activity so that it can be used more effectively in the rest of the nervous system. You would not want a radio if the volume dial would not turn in both directions. Both facilitation and inhibition are necessary to keep the vestibular system and the rest of the nervous system in balance.

When the facilitatory and inhibitory forces acting upon the vestibular system are not in balance, disorganization occurs. The information from the vestibular receptors does not flow to all of the locations in which it is needed. The pattern of all sensory processes is going to be different from the normal state. In some cases this may not be significant, while in others it may be very significant.

Influences upon the Eye and Neck Muscles

The muscles of the eye and neck play a particularly important role in organizing the vestibular system. Eye and neck muscle responses are among the infant's first sensory-motor functions, and they lay the ground-work for sensory-motor development in the rest of the body. Even in adults, much of the sensory-motor system works in a coordinated manner with the eyes and neck. A few impulses from the eyes or neck can trigger a whole sequence of changes in muscle contraction throughout the rest of the body.

Children with learning problems based on poor vestibular sensory processing often have difficulty following an object moving in front of their eyes, and also difficulty moving their eyes accurately from one spot to another. Instead of moving smoothly, their eyes may lag behind and then jerk to catch up. This makes playing ball, drawing a line with a piece of chalk, or reading a line of print very hard.

The vestibular system has the job of interpreting the orientation of our head and body so that we can know the meaning of information from our eyes. When we see something move in front of our eyes, our brain must know whether it is the object, our head, or our whole body that is moving. When something looks tilted, the brain needs to know whether the object is actually tilted, or our head is tilted, or the tilt is in our entire body. The eyes merely record whatever is in front of them; they do not tell the brain why things look the way they do.

The vestibular receptors tell the brain if the head is moving or tilted, but they do not provide information about the rest of the body. For the brain to know the relationship of object, head, and body, the gravity and movement sensations must interact with muscle and joint sensations, especially from the eyes and neck.

In many children with learning disabilities, these sensations are not integrated properly. The child may see normally in an eye test, but then run into furniture or walk off a step without seeing what he is doing. He sees the piece of furniture or the step, but he cannot tell how they relate to his body. He may overstep or understep the curb when he crosses the street, and sometimes turn his ankle. Some children walk right off the edge of a bed, as though they thought the bed and the floor were the same height.

The vestibular system also has the job of maintaining a stable visual field so that the things we see do not appear to flutter as we move. To do this, the vestibular system adjusts the eye and neck muscles to compensate for every movement of the head or body. A photographer does the same things with his hands so that he does not take a blurry picture.

Without adequate vestibular mechanisms to keep the eyes and head steady, it is very difficult for a child in school to follow the writing on the blackboard and copy it at his desk. We can appreciate his problem if we remember what it feels like to watch television when the picture flutters or wobbles, or to write something on paper while riding in a shaking car or boat. Two New York physicians, Jan Frank and Harold Levinson, conclude that lack of eye-neck-head stability is a major cause of *dysmetric dyslexia* or reading problems.

Nystagmus. After we spin around a few times and stop, our eyes move back and forth and the world seems to spin. This series of rapid back-and-forth eye movements is called *postrotary nystagmus.* Nystagmus is produced by reflex eye muscle contractions that are activated by the vestibular stimulation of spinning. At present, the duration of postrotary nystagmus is one of the better simple measurements of the efficiency or integrity of the vestibular system.

Sensory integration therapists test for nystagmus by placing the child on a rotating board and spinning him around. They then stop him and watch his eyes. If the nystagmus stops too soon, or does not occur at all, or is irregular, this means that the child's vestibular nuclei are not getting the proper amount of vestibular input or are not processing this input correctly. If the nystagmus lasts too long, the vestibular system is over-responding to vestibular input because there are not enough inhibitory forces acting on the vestibular system.

A number of studies in this country, in Australia, and in South America have shown that at least 50 percent of all children with learning or language problems have too short a duration of nystagmus. These findings suggest that some aspect of vestibular function is very important in meeting the demands of school work, and this aspect is not functioning adequately in many school children today. If the vestibular input is not acting upon the eye muscles, then it also is probably not providing other influences that are necessary for good auditory and visual processes. The processing of visual and auditory information is further discussed in Chapter VIII.

Influences on the Muscles of the Body

The vestibular nuclei send electrical messages down the spinal cord, and these messages join other messages to tell the muscles when and how to contract. This vestibular control of the muscles is entirely subconscious, and our voluntary muscle contractions are superimposed upon it. A continuous flow of impulses from the vestibular nuclei helps to generate muscle tone, especially in the muscles that straighten out the body and hold us in an upright position. As long as the vestibular system generates adequate muscle tone, we do not have to use much effort or concentration against the pull of gravity. If the vestibular system is disorganized, the muscles have low tone and the person gets tired quickly. This is the reason why many children with learning disabilities have trouble holding their heads up while sitting at a desk.

At the same time that messages are going down the spinal cord to the muscles, the muscles and joints are sending proprioceptive messages up to the vestibular nuclei and cerebellum. The vestibular nuclei and cerebellum constantly exchange information about sensory-motor processes. The cerebellum's job is to help us move smoothly, accurately, and with proper timing. If the vestibular nuclei and cerebellum do not process and integrate muscle and joint sensations, the child may stumble frequently and be clumsy in play. He may then become discouraged and sit around and watch television instead of playing. Without a great deal of full body play, the child does not get the kind of sensory input that is necessary to develop the brain as a whole. In addition, he will not have the experiences of mastery necessary for normal personality development.

Postural and Equilibrium Responses

Some of the most important functions of the vestibular system are carried out through nearby portions of the brain stem. The brain stem contains neural centers that—along with the help of other parts of the brain—organize many of our postural and equilibrium responses. These are automatic muscle contractions that keep our body balanced on two feet, support our arms in pushing and pulling things, and adjust our body to make our movements smooth. Good vestibular direction of postural and equilibrium responses is especially important when we are walking over rocks or on a hill, or when something pushes or pulls at our body. There are three additional, specific types of postural and equilibrium responses that are sometimes deficient in children with learning problems: postural background movements, cocontraction of muscles, and protective extension of arms or legs.

Postural background movements. When we reach for something, or push or pull with our hands, our trunk and legs automatically adjust themselves so that our arms do their job efficiently. These automatic adjustments are called postural background movements. We take these movements for granted, and think only of what we are doing with our arms and hands. However, the entire body must sense and move as a whole unit if the hands and arms are to do anything well.

Postural background movements are particularly important when we work at a desk. Some schoolteachers notice that learning disabled children do not move their trunks normally as they turn their heads or move their arms to write on paper. When the child does shift his body in the chair, he sometimes falls out of his seat. If his teacher tries to help him position his body, she may notice that he feels heavy or stiff. His body does not move freely, because the parts of his brain stem that direct postural background movements are not getting well-organized proprioceptive and vestibular messages. The same deficiency will prevent his moving normally when dancing or playing hopscotch.

Cocontraction. To hold the head steady and move it efficiently, all the muscles around the neck must be able to contract at the same time; this is called *cocontraction*. The muscles all around the trunk must be able to cocontract to hold the body steady so that it will not be easily pulled or pushed off balance. Cocontraction of muscles all around the shoulder, elbow, wrist, and finger joints is necessary to move well or work with tools.

Children with vestibular disorders often have poor cocontraction; they tend to contract muscles on just one side, and then on the other side a moment later. This makes the head and body like a table with wobbly legs.

Protective extension. Vestibular and proprioceptive impulses also interact to warn the brain of possible injury to the body when it is about to fall. When a well-organized child begins to fall during play, vestibular and proprioceptive input tells the brain that the body is approaching the ground, and this stimulates the brain to send out messages that extend or straighten the arms. This extension stops the fall and protects the face and chest. Children with poor organization of body and gravity sensations sometimes make no attempt to catch themselves when they fall, and so they often hurt their heads during play.

Vestibular-Reticular Interactions

The central portion of the brain stem is an extremely complex network of neurons known as the *reticular core*. (See Chapter 3.) The reticular core is the part of the brain responsible for the arousal of the nervous system. The reticular core sends impulses throughout the entire brain to awaken and alert the person. The vestibular system feeds a great many sensory impulses into this reticular arousal system.

Well-modulated vestibular activity is very important for maintaining a calm, alert state. We feel the calming effects of slow vestibular stimulation when we rock in a rocking chair, and feel the arousing effects of fast vestibular stimulation when riding in a roller coaster. The vestibular system also helps keep the level of arousal of the nervous system balanced. An underactive vestibular system contributes to hyperactivity and distractibility because of the lack of its modulating influence. In sensory integrative therapy vestibular stimulation is used to either quiet, stimulate, or organize a child's activity level.

In the early animals that were the ancestors of both human beings and present-day animals, the reticular core was *the* center for sensory integration. It was the part of the brain that unified all the other parts to function as a whole. Nature organized the reticular neurons to connect with neurons throughout the entire nervous system. Information entered the reticular core from everywhere, and reticular influences spread out widely and diffusely. A few neurons could do a lot of things.

The behavior of these animals was very simple, but it enabled survival. To catch a meal and avoid being one, the animal had to orient itself to space and move as one efficient unit. To help form these adaptive responses, the vestibular system evolved very early, and continued to evolve in conjunction with the reticular system throughout the eons leading to the appearance of man. Our vestibular and reticular systems still have most of those widespread neural connections that evolved in early animals.

Simple vestibular and reticular functions were operating long before the systems for muscle, joint, and complex auditory and visual sensory processing evolved. These newer systems evolved out of the old reticular core. The vestibular system had a great deal of influence over the evolution of these newer systems, and this primal influence is still operating in our brain today. This is one reason why therapy involving vestibular stimulation is effective in improving language and reading.

Interactions with Other Senses

In the brain, almost everything influences just about everything else; this makes sensory integration more complex than we can ever comprehend. But if the senses did not interact so much, we would not have evolved brains that can think and reason, and we probably would not even have survived.

As the proprioceptive system evolved, it took on the job of helping the brain to modulate the vestibular system. Muscle and joint sensations enable the brain to use vestibular input effectively. For this reason, therapists sometimes have children with vestibular disorders push, pull, lift, and carry heavy items. These heavy work patterns contract a lot of muscles and compress many joints in the body, and thereby provide input that helps to inhibit the excess vestibular activity that is causing problems in the brain.

All types of sensory input come together in the vestibular nuclei and reticular core of the brain stem. Then some of them flow up to the thalamus at the top of the brain stem for further integration. Sensory integration is completed in the cerebral hemispheres, where the information from the distance receptors—the eyes and ears—is processed into precise perceptions and associations.

The vestibular system forms a link between the body senses and the sensations of distant events. The visual areas of the cerebral cortex receive so much input from the vestibular system that proper development of vision would be impossible without adequate vestibular function throughout the years of childhood. Less is known about how vestibular activity influences the auditory processes in the cerebral cortex, but it is known that vestibular activity is important for auditory precessing in the brain stem. As we described in Chapter III, the two systems evolved together in the bones of the inner ears, with their sensory inputs traveling side-by-side in a single nerve to the brain stem. They are "neighbors" and they "talk" to each other.

Relating to Space

Vestibular information is processed along with proprioception and vision in the cerebral cortex to let us know where we are in space. This knowledge then passes to the motor regions of the cortex, which direct us in moving our bodies and manipulating objects. A kindergarten child with a vestibular problem may have trouble pasting one piece of paper on another, because his brain cannot line up the two pieces in space. An older child is likely to have trouble spacing his letters as he writes them.

It is not uncommon for children with vestibular problems to run in the wrong direction when they are playing a team sport. The child may not want to jump into a swimming pool, because he is not quite sure how far he is from the water. Such problems are very frustrating for the child and lead to poor self-esteem and unhappy relationships with other children.

In more severe cases, the child does not want to play outside alone. He may feel lost even in his own backyard. His brain cannot sense the spatial relationships among trees and bushes and the house and his own body. He may be afraid that he will not be able to find his way back into the house. One man reported that sometimes when he was sitting in a chair, he suddenly felt that the chair was sideways halfway up the wall with him still in it. In his car, he would feel that the car was traveling along upside-down.

A vestibular disorder may interfere with social relationships. The person has a hard time knowing how close to stand to other people and often offends by standing too close. He may have trouble judging where people are, especially in a crowd. He cannot tell how much room he needs to go around people, and often bumps into them. Without the space perception that comes from sensations of the body and gravity, it is difficult to visualize space. The person may know how to get somewhere himself, but not be able to give directions to someone else.

Space perception improves during therapy involving vestibular stimulation. Children begin to climb and relate themselves to vertical space. Other children, who are too disorganized to climb, begin to move furniture all around the house, much to the dismay of their mothers. The child is following his inner drive to explore space and learn about the relationships between his body and that space.

Influences on Emotional Development and Behavior
Few people think of emotions as functions of the nervous system. However, there is a neurological basis for every feeling of fear, anger, sadness, joy, and even love. The limbic system is the part of the cerebral hemispheres that generates emotionally based behavior. For emotions to be "balanced," the limbic system must receive well-modulated input from the senses. Experiments have shown that without vestibular stimulation during infancy, animals often grow up to be hostile, aggressive, or withdrawn. There is also evidence that some types of autism and schizophrenia are related to certain disorders of the vestibular system.

One of the most basic of all human relationships is our relationship to the gravitational field of the earth. This relationship is far more primal than the mother-child relationship. Sensory integration of the vestibular system does give us "gravitational security"—the trust that we are firmly connected to the earth and will always have a safe place to stand. Gravitational security is the foundation upon which we build our interpersonal relationships.

Normal children spend much of their time developing their relationship to gravity. First the baby lifts up his head and finds out that gravity makes it heavy. With each new movement, he learns what gravity can do and what he can do. He learns that the pull of gravity never, ever changes its direction or strength. He discovers that there is nothing on this planet that can avoid gravity, but that by adapting to gravity he can stand up, climb a tree, or throw a ball in the air. Gravitational security is so vital to emotional health that nature has given us a strong inner drive to explore gravity and master it. Because this inner drive is so strong, a child will intuitively do whatever is necessary to develop his vestibular system. Mothers have always used rocking to calm down a distressed baby. The cradle is our symbol for the peace and serenity of infancy. Both young and old find that rocking chairs and swings reduce anxiety and emotional upset. Children love playground equipment and amusement park rides, because swinging, sliding, climbing, and riding a see-saw or merry-go-round or roller coaster provide so much vestibular stimulation. Skiing, flying, high diving, and fast driving are emotionally gratifying for quite a few adolescents and adults, and just about everyone enjoys some type of body movement. Long periods of rocking are common among institutionalized children and monkeys deprived of their mothers. Many children in sensory integrative therapy ride on a piece of equipment for long periods of time, indicating that they have a great need for vestibular input.

Because gravitational security is so essential to our nature, we take it for granted. Therefore, when something goes wrong in the neural functions that relate us to gravity, most people attribute the resulting problem to some other cause. A psychologist traces an emotional problem back to conflicts in childhood, but sometimes the problem can be traced even further back to poor processing of vestibular sensations during fetal life and infancy.

If the child's relationship to the earth is not secure, then all other relationships fail to develop optimally. Even the most loving mother cannot "reach" her child if the earth is not a safe place for him to be. Children with vestibular disorders seem to be missing something vital, as if they were "lost in space." Sometimes they cannot follow their inner drive because they are so afraid of what might happen to them. Therefore the child misses many of the sensory-motor experiences that are needed as building blocks for mature emotions and behavior.

Influences on the Digestive Tract

Anyone who has been motion sick in a car or on a boat knows the close association between the vestibular system and the digestive tract. When there is more vestibular input than the brain can organize, the digestive centers in the brain stem are upset. This stops the movement of food through the digestive tract and gives us feelings of nausea and queasiness. Such a response is normal during or after excessive movement. *Not* to feel dizzy or sick to the stomach after a great deal of movement may be a sign that the vestibular system is not processing all of the sensations from the inner ears. Children with vestibular disorder also frequently have difficulty in developing bowel and bladder control.

Influences on Academic Learning

Reading, writing, and computing are not "the basics"; they require that the brain process very detailed sensations and engage in precise motor and mental responses. The visual system must distinguish the very small differences among letters of the alphabet, numbers, and punctuation marks. The child must have good space perception to see the difference between *41* and *14* or between *was* and *saw*. His cerebral cortex must process the visual input according to spelling and grammatical rules that are both arbitrary and variable. For the cortex to do this, all the parts of the brain that deal with language must communicate with all the parts that deal with visual perception and memory. Writing is even more complicated, for in addition to all of the above, the brain must process hand and finger sensations, compare them with memories of how the hands and fingers are supposed to feel when they write, and then organize the muscle contractions that move the pencil.

None of these brain functions can work well if the brain cannot receive and process sensations from movement and gravity. If a child has a vestibular disorder, many of the sensory-motor patterns in his brain will be disorganized, and he will have no way to remember what a printed word means or how to write that word himself. The cruelest thing a teacher can say to a learning disabled child is, "You could do it if only you would try!" How can a child read if he can't even connect what he sees with what he hears? How can he write his name if he has to concentrate on keeping himself in his chair? These sensory-motor abilities are the real "basics," and learning problems will continue until the schools pay attention to their development. Some children have acquired the basics through normal development, and they are ready to learn to read at five or six years of age; but many other children have not been able to master the basics because of a neurological irregularity. To try to teach them to read at age six is to invite failure and misery for the child. The child usually strikes back, and is then considered a behavior problem.

The Underreactive Vestibular System

There are two types of vestibular disorders that commonly interfere with learning and behavior: the brain either underreacts to vestibular input or it overreacts. Using the analogy of a radio, either the volume is set too low or it is set too high. When the facilitatory and inhibitory forces of the brain do not balance vestibular activity, neither vestibular input nor the input from the other senses can be used easily for producing adaptive responses. In the rest of this chapter, we shall discuss these two types of dysfunction.

When a sensory integration therapist evaluates a child, she looks for the responses that the vestibular system should produce. The responses of the eyes and body are easiest to observe. Those of the eyes are most purely of vestibular origin. The duration and regularity of postrotary nystagmus is a good indication of the efficiency of some part of the vestibular system. When a child's nystagmus does not last as long as it should or is absent altogether, we know that he is not processing vestibular input in at least one very important neural pathway and is probably deficient in other vestibular functions also. Many of these children do not become dizzy or queasy, even after many minutes of spinning, and this is another indication that the vestibular input is not getting through to where it should go.

In the beginning of this chapter, we imagined four children walking a curb. The first child had a normal vestibular system. The second and third children had underreactive vestibular systems and would show short duration of nystagmus after rotation. The second child's underreactive vestibular system produced a "vestibular-bilateral" problem that made learning to read very difficult. The third child's underreactive vestibular processing interfered with his speech and language development.

What Is a Vestibular-Bilateral Disorder?

The symptoms of a vestibular-bilateral disorder are very subtle. These children are often considered completely normal until they enter school and have trouble with reading, arithmetic, or other academic work. School psychologists who are not trained to see the physical symptoms of a sensory integrative disorder often say that such a child has dyslexia or word-blindness. Other professionals may say that there is nothing at all wrong, or that the problem is really an emotional one.

Children with vestibular-bilateral disorders often have average or above-average IQs, so why do they have difficulty with school work? Although they are intelligent, they cannot use that intelligence easily when learning to read or compute. Some part of the meaning of the words and numbers gets jumbled in their brains.

They respond very poorly to the efforts of special education teachers. Children with other kinds of learning disabilities are able to take advantage of special education or tutoring, but the child with a vestibular-bilateral problem cannot very well. On the other hand, they usually respond very well to sensory integrative therapy, and after a year of therapy, many with vestibular-bilateral disorders can learn more easily, although it may still be difficult. To attack this type of learning disorder with just academic work is placing the cart before the horse. These children need sensory integrative therapy along with school work.

Eye muscle and postural responses. A reading or math problem is only one symptom of the irregularity in brain function that shortens the duration of nystagmus. If the eye muscles do not get enough input to produce a normal nystagmus after rotation, the child will also have difficulty using his eyes to follow a moving object and to look from one spot to another. Very few people notice these deficiencies in eye movements, but the sensory integration therapist is trained to see them.

Postural responses may also be deficient. Because the vestibular nuclei do not receive enough input, they cannot send enough impulses down the spinal cord to the muscles that extend the neck, arms, back, and legs. The child may have trouble holding his head up while sitting or may become tired easily during play. If your child has this problem, you can see it by having him lie on his tummy and asking him to raise both ends of his body and hold them up. Many children with vestibular-bilateral disorders cannot hold this "airplane position" for more than a few seconds.

Sometimes, when these children start to fall, they do not seem to notice that they are falling, and they make no attempt to regain their balance. As they fall to the ground, they do not extend their arms to protect themselves. During therapy, one child was lying on a large ball and started to fall off. I said, "Get ready to catch yourself, you are going to fall." The child answered, "But which way am I going to fall?" and was on the floor before I could answer him.

Children with vestibular-bilateral disorders often find it difficult and frightening to learn to ride a bicycle. The child cannot be sure that he will shift his weight properly and make the correct turns to avoid obstacles in his path. In general, these children rarely experience the thrill of "being good" at games or sports, and they do not feel confident or happy like other children. Some of the boys with these problems try to gain approval by being the class clown and falling down to amuse the other children. Even though most children with this type of deficit are clumsy, some do develop normal motor coordination. Normal coordination does not assure normal reading ability, however.

"Faster, faster!" The child with an underreactive vestibular system does not process enough vestibular sensations, and so he does not get the "nourishment" that other children get from body movement and play. However, he does have an inner drive to develop his brain. In addition, the child often does not get dizzy or nauseous until after he has had an enormous amount of movement. It is not surprising, therefore, that these children often like to ride a merry-go-round or roller coaster for a much longer time than other children. In therapy, they often want to go faster and faster on the moving equipment.

One child, in a net swing for the first time, said, "I could do this for a million years," which tells us how much his vestibular system was in need of stimulation. In therapy, these children receive a great deal of swinging and spinning in an effort to activate the vestibular system. However, only an occupational or physical therapist who is trained in sensory integrative therapy and who knows the child's nervous system very well should spin or swing a child for a long time. One of the most dangerous things you can do is spin a child whose brain is dysfunctional. Spinning may reduce breathing and blood pressure and cause a loss of consciousness. If the child is even slightly prone to have seizures, spinning or swinging may bring on a seizure.

Bilateral integration. A child with underreactive vestibular responses often has poor integration of the two sides of the body. He has difficulty coordinating his left and right hands. He is easily confused by directions or instructions, especially when he has no time to think about which side is which. When you ask him to turn left, he may go to the right. He has trouble dancing or playing a drum, because his hands and feet do not work well together, and cannot follow a rhythm.

As he becomes older, the child may use other parts of his brain to compensate for poor vestibular functioning. He may learn to rely upon thought processes to tell the difference between left and right. Then he may appear to have normal left-right discrimination, although he still has difficulty when the task is new or unusual. Compensation by other parts of the brain is never as efficient as the natural function of the part that is designed to do the job.

In Chapter 4, we discussed the specialization of each side of the body and brain for different functions. An underreactive vestibular system often interferes with specialization. The child develops similar skills with each hand and each cerebral hemisphere. Instead of using just one hand for fine motor work such as writing or using tools, he tends to use his right hand on the right side of his body and his left hand on his left. He may be considered ambidextrous, but actually he is not especially skilled with either hand. Or he may become left-handed, while genetically he is meant to be right-handed.

Meanwhile, inside his brain, both of his cerebral hemispheres are doing similar things instead of specializing for greater overall efficiency. The child tries to develop language in both hemispheres, but does not do very well in either one. This may cause difficulties in speech, reading, and writing. Speech may be late in coming, and the child usually understands more than he can speak. Once speech does develop, it is usually normal, or close to normal, in quality and quantity. Lack of lateralization of skills in children with vestibular-bilateral disorders leads us to speculate that these children do not have normal communication between their two hemispheres. When the two sides of the brain cannot communicate, they cannot function in a natural, efficient way.

A Checklist for Vestibular-Bilateral Disorder

The following is a summary of the major symptoms of this disorder. The first two are characteristic and define this particular disorder. The other symptoms are found in some children, but not in others; they may also be seen in other types of sensory integrative disorder.

1. The child appears to be normal, healthy, and normally intelligent, but has trouble learning to read or do mathematics.
2. The duration of nystagmus following rotation is shorter than normal.
3. The child is not really good at sports or does not enjoy them. Throwing or catching a ball may be difficult.
4. Large movements are clumsy. The child stumbles and falls more frequently than others his age, and sometimes makes no attempt to catch himself.
5. When you try to help the child balance himself on a narrow surface or a large ball, he feels heavy, like a sack of potatoes.
6. When the child lies on his stomach, he cannot easily hold up his head, arms, and legs all at the same time.
7. He cannot hold his head still and steady when someone tries to move it around in every direction.
8. His hands do not work well together, nor do his feet.

9. He does not have normal hand dominance. He may be considered ambidextrous, but usually he is not very skillful with either hand.
10. The child sometimes gets right and left confused, especially when he has no time to think about which hand is which.
11. When learning to write, he reverses letters like "b" and "d" more often than his classmates. Sometimes he reads words backwards: "saw for "was."
12. He does not tolerate stress well and is often frustrated.
13. The child does not think well of himself. It is hard to feel all right about yourself when the most important part of you—your brain— is not working entirely right. Sometimes there is a definite emotional or behavior problem.

Vestibular-Language Disorders

Communication through language is to some extent an end product of sensory integration. The vestibular system is a major organizer of sensation in all the other sensory channels, and so it contributes to the development of word understanding and speech. This insight came from findings that children with language disorders showed improvement in their speech and language after sensory integrative therapy, although the therapy did not include language training.

Therapists have found that children with problems in articulation, speech, and language often have a short duration of post-rotary nystagmus. Stilwell, Crowe, and McCallum tested the nystagmus of children in an Illinois speech and hearing center and compared them with normal children. They found that 70 percent of the children with language disorders had nystagmus of shorter duration than 70 percent of normal children. Those having difficulty in symbolic use of language and syntax had the lowest duration of nystagmus. Of the children we imagined in the introduction, the third child has a speech disorder with underreactive vestibular function.

It is generally agreed that the functions of higher parts of the brain, such as the cerebral cortex, are partially dependent upon lower subcortical functions. The language center in the left cerebral hemisphere (in right-handed individuals) is part of a larger network involving other parts of the cortex and also subcortical integrating centers. For speech to develop and occur, the higher and lower centers must constantly interact. If vestibular processes in the lower centers are deficient, the higher areas will have a hard time producing normal speech.

Of course, there are many other reasons why a child might have trouble with language. When speech does not develop on schedule, the child's postrotary nystagmus should be tested by a sensory integration therapist.

It is easy to see that vestibular input has some facilitatory effect on vocalization. Almost every child yells and screams when he is riding on a roller coaster or playing very actively. Often nonspeaking children make more sounds than usual during vestibular stimulation in therapy. It is as if the brain needed a certain amount of vestibular input to produce sounds, and the movements of daily life did not supply the amount needed in these children.

I once evaluated a six-year-old boy who was reported to be quite uncooperative. I asked him to choose which of two blocks would fit into a formboard. He just sat there, neither moving nor responding to anything I said. Eventually I gave up and decided that I would at least test the child for postrotary nystagmus. After being spun around, the child showed almost no nystagmus; but then he voluntarily got up, went to the table, and started to speak and put the blocks into the formboard! After a few minutes, he stopped working. I brought him back to the rotating board and spun him some more, and he then returned to the table to continue the tests. This cycle continued several times until the testing was completed. It seems that this child could be cooperative only after his brain was facilitated by vestibular input.

Children with speech and language disorders along with vestibular dysfunction usually also have difficulties in body movement and motor planning. Disorders in motor planning are discussed in Chapter VI.

Not all speech and language disorders are associated with vestibular dysfunction. Some communication deficits seem to be the result of poor function in the speech centers of the left cerebral hemisphere. In children with this type of language disorder, the problem is not caused by poor sensory integration, and these children do not usually benefit from sensory integrative therapy.

Overreactive Vestibular Responses

Sensation is "food" for the nervous system, but too much of anything causes problems. The normal brain processes vestibular sensations and uses their information to form an adaptive response. To use vestibular input, the brain must inhibit impulses that are not useful. Some brains, however, cannot inhibit or modulate vestibular activity, and so they overreact to vestibular stimulation.

Usually the child with overreactive vestibular responses has a longer duration of postrotary nystagmus than normal. However, sometimes these children do have normal or even short duration of nystagmus. It is important to remember that the vestibular system has many pathways and many different functions; some of these functions may be underactive, while others are overactive and still others normal.

There are two types of hypersensitivity to vestibular input: *gravitational insecurity* and *intolerance to movement*. In the former, the disorder seems to be in the part of the brain modulating input from the gravity receptors, and so the position of the head or body may make the child uncomfortable, even if he is not moving. In the latter, the part of the brain processing input from the semicircular canal receptors is more involved, and so movement causes the discomfort.

Gravitational Insecurity

Extreme movement or falling will cause fear in just about everyone. However, some people have an excessive emotional reaction to vestibular sensations, even when there is no danger of falling. The fear has little to do with the actual status of the body; instead it comes from a "mistake" in vestibular processing within the brain. Sensory integration therapists call this problem *postural insecurity* or *gravitational insecurity*.

The fourth child mentioned in the beginning of this chapter is gravitationally insecure. He is afraid to get on the curb, but does so when his mother encourages him and holds his hand. However, his balance and motor coordination are better than those of the two children with underreactive vestibular responses, and he does not physically need his mother's helping hand. He could walk the curb by himself, but his brain cannot perceive that he has that ability. Since he does not stumble or fall, it is not easy to see that he has a problem. Gravitational insecurity does not, in itself, interfere with academic learning, and so the child may do fine in school—unless he has other neurologic problems in addition to his overreaction to vestibular input.

The gravitationally insecure child feels fear, anxiety, or distress whenever he is in a position to which he is not accustomed, or when he tries to assume such a position, or when someone else tries to control his movement or position. He is particularly threatened when other people move him. He may not even allow others to stand nearby when he is working, as if he thought that they might try to move him by surprise. Swings, merry-go-rounds, and other playthings that move the body in nonordinary ways may terrify him, but he may be able to tolerate them if he is in the security of a parent's lap. Turning a corner rapidly in an automobile may be disconcerting.

He spends much of his time worrying about falling and goes to considerable lengths to avoid falling, even though he seldom does fall. In contrast, the child with a vestibular bilateral problem may fall frequently, but often takes no precautions against falling and usually shows no emotional response. One gravitationally insecure child had her hands firmly on the floor, but her legs on a wobbly piece of equipment. Instead of simply crawling off, she called out, "I'm falling, I'm falling!"

A primal threat. The gravitationally insecure child feels a primal threat in the pull of gravity. His reluctance to move is not willful, and nothing that you tell him can change his insecurity. It will not do any good to encourage him with rewards. His fear is not rational; it comes from deep inside his brain where words and rewards have no effect. This child is in sheer misery, and his misery increases as adults and other children ignore his needs and expect him to move like other children.

He feels safest when both feet are firmly on the floor. An eight-year-old girl would not step over a rope one foot above the floor; instead she scooted underneath. Jumping may be very threatening, and some of these children "jump" without their feet leaving the floor. They are reluctant to lie in a horizontal position anywhere but on the floor or a bed, and may resist lying on a table or platform.

Some gravitationally insecure people are afraid of walking up or down hill, or over ground that is rocky or bumpy. They hold the banister carefully when going up or down stairs. They do not like to walk on curbs, climb, or ride on things or animals. Leaning over backward from a sitting position may be threatening.

Since the problem is oversensitivity to input from the gravity receptors, the position of the head is critical for these persons. Adult women with gravitational insecurity have complained that they feel uncomfortable cleaning house, because they must lower their heads under and around furniture. Holding the head upside-down provides the greatest stimulation to the gravity receptors, and is particularly threatening to those who cannot modulate this input. Gravitationally insecure children avoid somersaults, and rough-housing is not pleasurable for them.

These children often demand constant physical support from a parent or therapist. Their reluctance to be on their own severely limits their play and does not allow them opportunities to mature like other children. If you have a child who is gravitationally insecure, your friends and neighbors may say that you are being overprotective and should encourage him to grow up. They say this because they do not realize that your child cannot modulate the most basic of all sensations. The best thing you can do for your child is to respect his needs and do whatever you can to gradually build his sense of trust.

Our relationship to gravity is our most important source of security. The gravitationally insecure child probably feels that any body movement might send him hurtling off into other space. A little bit of movement may make him feel "spacy" or "all spaced out." One person, after a movement experience that most people would not find uncomfortable, said, "I felt as though I were leaving the earth and I would never get back!" There is no more primal threat.

If the child-earth relationship is not secure, then all other relationships are apt to be less than optimal. Thus gravitational insecurity may damage every aspect of a person's life. People will not notice his fear, and will find him "hard to get along with." They may blame or punish him for what his brain makes him do. Other children call him "chicken." Teachers do not understand why words do not reassure him. To do things with other people, he must encounter fears they do not feel or understand.

To avoid or reduce the distress, he will try to manipulate his environment and other people. This makes him seem obstinate and uncooperative. As a small child, he learns that big adults will move him about without any respect for his oversensitive vestibular system. He then learns ways to control adults and keep them away. The child does not know which situations will be terrifying and which ones will be all right, so he has to control everything as much as possible. Adults then consider this an undesirable personality trait; they try to be the "boss" and force the child to stop being manipulative. The child then suffers even greater misery.

Cecilia Rothschild spoke for many when she wrote:

Playground of Fear

My life unfolded on the playground
With all of its pain and joy.
The fears and doubts of myself
Came into play—there in that make-believe, all too real world.

I was lost in the jungle gym,
Unsure of myself—confused,
My direction uncertain.
And no laughter came from me
As I wound my way round this labyrinth of terror.

I climbed up the steps of the giant slide,
Frozen by what lay ahead of me—
Unable to turn back.
And no laughter came from me
As I plunged blindly ahead, uncertain of my fate.

I scampered to the see-saw
Expectations of fun—excitement,
All turned sour in mid-air as I hung suspended in space.
And no laughter came from me
As I toppled from my dream to meet a harsh reality below.

I jumped on a swing
Prepared for an exhilarating experience—flying.
When the others pushed me beyond my security—laughing—the
     speed blurring all chance for reason,
And no laughter came from me,
As I clung to the hope of a speedy end to my anguish.

I came, in the end, to meet the challenge of the metal rings—
     hopeful—here control was mine alone.
But the cold gray steel gave off no shine that summer day.
And only tears came from me
As I was struck on the head in an unconscious moment—
A cruel and bitter message of my helplessness.

So I ran from the playground of fear—
This make-believe, all too real world,
Home where these games of life continued to be played out.
And no laughter came from me.

29 April 1973*

What's wrong with the nervous system? As with any sensory integrative disorder, we can only conjecture about what is going on inside the child's brain. At this time, we believe that the input from the gravity receptors is not properly modulated. Gravity sensations enter the brain continuously as long as we are alive, and they increase when the head moves from the normal position to which we are accustomed. Thus the gravitationally insecure child can find relief from his terror only by holding his head as still as possible, by making sure that it does not get into unusual positions, and by keeping his feet firmly on the ground so he will know where he is in relation to space.

---

*Printed by permission of the author.

Part of the problem may lie in insufficient muscle and joint sensory input, which is needed to modulate vestibular activity. If an infant cannot move about enough to integrate vestibular and proprioceptive sensations, or if he has some neural disorder that prevents this integration, his brain may fail to develop enough of an inhibitory influence over the vestibular system.

The neurologic condition that causes gravitational insecurity does not, in itself, interfere with academic performance, although the resulting distress may do so. Gravitational insecurity is often seen in children with other, more extensive neurologic irregularities that do interfere with the learning process. These irregularities often make it difficult for the person to organize himself and focus on a task.

These are very anxious people, and they can easily become neurotic or emotionally ill. Unfortunately psychotherapists may treat their anxiety as though it were a personality defect rather than a neurologic disorder.

The urge to overcome gravitational insecurity. Every human being has a primal inner drive to develop a satisfactory relationship with gravity. The normal child follows that urge by creeping, playing, climbing, jumping, and putting himself in every conceivable body position. He learns what he can do, and what gravity can do, and eventually comes to terms with gravity.

The child with gravitational insecurity has this urge, but his emotional reactions prevent his following it. In sensory integrative therapy, the environment is designed to enable normal responses to emerge. The therapist knows how to guide and not push. Thus the inner drive almost always appears in the child during therapy and enables him to overcome much of his insecurity.

One girl spent many months trying to master the feeling of having her head upside-down. After therapy, she would go home and sit in her mother's lap with her head lowered into an upside-down position.

A Checklist for Gravitational Insecurity

Here is a summary of the symptoms of gravitational insecurity. Not all symptoms are seen in any one child. Also, some of these symptoms are present in children who do not have sensory integrative disorders.

1. When his feet leave the ground, the child becomes anxious or struggles to keep his feet down. He may cooperate if he is assisted by someone he trusts.
2. He has an unnatural fear of falling or of heights.
3. He dislikes having his head upside-down, such as in somersaults, rolling on the floor, or rough-housing.
4. He does not have fun on playground equipment or with moving toys.
5. He avoids jumping down from a higher surface to a lower one.
6. The child is particularly slow at unusual movements, such as getting into a car, moving from the front seat to the back, or walking up or down hill or over bumpy ground.
7. He may take a long time to learn to go up or down stairs, and uses the banister more than other children.

8. He may avoid climbing, even simple climbing when he can hang on with both hands.
9. He is afraid of walking on a raised surface; it seems high to him, although not to others.
10. He feels as if he will lose his balance when he is spun around.
11. Going around corners rapidly in a car frightens him.
12. The child appears to be judging space inaccurately, although the problem actually is that he cannot handle movement within that space.
13. He is alarmed if suddenly pushed backward while seated.

Intolerance to Movement

Some children's overreactive vestibular systems feel great discomfort during rapid movement or spinning in circles. They are not necessarily threatened by movement; it just makes them uncomfortable. These children are apt to become car sick more easily than other children. They become nauseated more quickly when playing on things that move, such as a merry-go-round, or in therapy on equipment designed to provide vestibular stimulation. Some extremely sensitive individuals even feel sick when they watch someone else or an object spin, for this stimulates an eye reflex that in turn activates the vestibular nuclei.

It seems likely that the part of the nervous system that modulates input from the semicircular canals is not functioning properly in these children. Spinning activates the semicircular canals more than any other stimulus, but has a lesser effect on the gravity receptors. One might think that gravitational insecurity and intolerance to movement would go hand-in-hand, and they sometimes do, although not always. It is often difficult to tell them apart.

Since the vestibular input generated by movement overstimulates the nervous system in these children and upsets their digestion, one might think that it would cause postrotary nystagmus to be of long duration. While this is often the case, it is not necessarily so; the vestibular system is so incredibly complex that all sorts of variations in function are possible.

Intolerance to movement has not been studied as much as gravitational insecurity, and so we do not know for sure whether it interferes with academic performance or behavior. Most therapists have the impression that it does not affect academic work, but is more likely to interfere with personality development. There is not a great deal of spinning in school or in life, and so the child may avoid it pretty easily without missing out on very much. However, the neural disorder that makes spinning very uncomfortable may make other types of movement slightly uncomfortable. If a child cannot feel pleasure when he moves, he will miss out on a lot of the satisfaction of childhood, and he will give himself fewer opportunities to develop sensory integration. As we get older, we naturally have less tolerance to movement than we did as children, so lesser enjoyment of movement in an adult does not indicate a neurological problem.

REFERENCES

Ayres, A. Jean. Sensorimotor foundations of academic ability. In W.M. Cruickshank & D.P. Hallahan (Eds.), *Perceptual and learning disabilities in children*, Vol. 2. Syracuse, N.Y.: Syracuse University Press, 1975.

Ayres, A. Jean. Learning disabilities and the vestibular system. *Journal of Learning Disabilities*, 1978, *11*, 18-29.

de Quiros, Julio B., & Schrager, Orlando L. *Neuropsychological fundamentals in learning disabilities*. San Rafael, Calif.: Academic Therapy Publications, 1978.

Frank, Jan, & Levinson, Harold N. Dysmetric dyslexia and dyspraxia: Synopsis of a continuing research project. *Academic Therapy*, 1975-76, *11*(2), 133-143.

Ottenbacher, Kenneth. Identifying vestibular processing dysfunction in learning disabled children. *American Journal of Occupational Therapy*, 1978, *32*, 217-221.

Steinberg, Margaret, & Rendle-Short, John. Vestibular dysfunction in young children with minor neurological impairment. *Developmental Medicine and Child Neurology*, 1977, *19*, 639-651.

Stilwell, Janet M., Crowe, Terry K., & McCallum, L.W. Postrotary nystagmus duration as a function of communication disorders. *American Journal of Occupational Therapy*, 1978, *32*, 222-228.

CHAPTER 6

DEVELOPMENTAL DYSPRAXIA: A MOTOR PLANNING PROBLEM

If you stop and think about what man can do, you will realize that everything is either a movement or a process in which movement is required for the expression of that process; for instance, thoughts are expressed through movement. Without movement, we could not take care of ourselves, go where we want to go, or communicate with others. It is no wonder that most of the brain is involved in preparing body movements.

Movement is something we can see; we especially notice it when it is poorly done. Because so many different brain processes are involved in movement, many different brain disorders can cause poor coordination. One type of poor coordination that is the result of sensory integrative dysfunction is a deficit in motor planning. This type of sensory processing problem is called *developmental dyspraxia* or, if it is fairly severe, *apraxia*.

In Chapter 3, we discussed motor planning or *praxis*, which is the ability to plan and carry out an unfamiliar action. The dyspraxic child is slow and inefficient at motor planning; the apraxic child can hardly motor plan at all. However, these children may have normal intelligence and muscles. The problem is in the "bridge" between their intellect and their muscles.

Developmental dyspraxia is one of the most common manifestations of sensory integrative dysfunction in children with learning disorders or minimal brain dysfunction. Recognizing and understanding it is not easy. To help us understand dyspraxia, we shall look first at other types of poor motor coordination and compare dyspraxia with these other problems.

Types of Movement and Movement Disorders

We shall consider five aspects of movement: (1) smooth control of movement, such as in picking up a pin; (2) postural reactions, such as rolling over or balancing on one foot; (3) patterns of movement that are programmed into the central nervous system, such as crawling or walking;

91

(4) specific motor skills, such as tying an overhand knot or writing the alphabet; and (5) motor planning.

Smooth Control

If the neurons that carry motor messages from the brain to the muscles are not working well, the muscles do not receive a smooth flow of directions and therefore contract in a jerky, involuntary manner. These *choreoathetoid movements* are a result of insufficient inhibition in the motor tracts. They are like static on a radio—extra noise that should not be there.

Very mild involuntary jerky movements are often seen in children with minimal brain dysfunction when the child tries to do fine work, such as putting a small peg into a small hole. Jerkiness makes him spill his food after the age at which most children can feed themselves neatly. Later on it discourages him from using a crayon or pencil and from playing with small toys. As far as we know it does not directly hinder mental work. However, even mild choreoathetoid movements that cannot easily be seen will interfere with handwriting and sports. These involuntary jerky movements are probably *not* a result of sensory integrative dysfunction, and they require another form of therapy.

Postural Reactions

A very important aspect of coordination is the ability to change position and move from one place to another without losing balance. We also have to move our trunk and shift our weight so that arms can operate away from our body. In the first few weeks after birth, postural reactions help the infant lift up his head, roll over, and get up on his hands and knees. These early postural reactions lay the foundation for balancing and equilibrium responses that develop later on.

All of these movements depend upon the integration of both motor messages and sensory input from the muscles, joints, vestibular system, and, to a lesser extent, the skin. They are semi-automatic or reflex motions that do not require thinking, and they work better when we don't think about them. Because they are very dependent upon sensory processing, they are often deficient in children with sensory integrative dysfunctions. These postural disorders are discussed in detail in Chapter 5.

Centrally Programmed Movement

Have you ever wondered how spiders can move their six legs so quickly with such good coordination? They do not have to plan these movements; they merely "turn on" the part of their nervous system that has been "programmed" to carry out the right pattern. The human being also has patterns of movement that are programmed into his central nervous system. Creeping and walking are the best examples of central programming in man.

Parents usually do not get down on their hands and knees to teach their child how to creep. The child innately knows how to do this, and will do so when his nervous system reaches that level of maturity—assuming that the child develops in a normal manner. Even though the child has a built-in knowledge of how to creep, he still must use a little motor planning when he first learns this new action.

Walking is centrally programmed, but talking requires motor planning, unless the person is a very good speaker or the conversation is simple. The brain with normal praxis (motor planning skill) can organize talking at the same time as walking. However, most people cannot tie an unfamiliar, complicated knot while talking about something else, because both actions require motor planning and the brain cannot handle two different motor plans at the same time.

When we first learn to sit down in a chair, we have to motor plan walking up to it, turning around, and placing our body just right on the chair. Later on we can rely upon our memory of the motor directions to sit down without thinking about our movements. When we see a child sit nicely at six months, and later see that he cannot learn motor skills, we suspect that his postural reactions and central programming are all right, but that his motor planning ability is poor.

Most children with minimal brain dysfunction have no trouble with centrally programmed movements, because these do not require complex sensory integration. Problems in executing centrally programmed movements are more apt to be seen in children with cerebral palsy or other severe irregularities in the motor tracts of the brain.

Motor Skills

Each of us has a "library" of skills that we can perform whenever we need them. A skill is something that we initially had to motor plan in order to learn, but now we do it spontaneously. When a child first learns to tie his shoes, he has to pay attention to his fingers and the shoelaces; that attention makes it motor planning. After he has motor planned the knot successfully a few times, it "sinks into" his brain and becomes a skill.

Once a skill has been learned, it no longer requires motor planning or conscious attention. Skills are integrated into the overall operation of the brain, and so they emerge spontaneously. A good example is typing. The beginner uses every bit of conscious attention to find the keys, while the skilled typist simply allows his brain to do the work. His brain organizes the contractions of his finger muscles so automatically that he does not have to look at the keys or think about what he is typing. After many years of using the neurons of the brain for typing, this skill can become as automatic as walking.

Skills require no motor planning as long as the situation is familiar. However, when something unusual occurs, such as when the skilled typist works on a typewriter on which some of the keys are placed differently, these skills must be assisted by some motor planning. Most adults have the skill of buttoning clothes, but most motor plan if the button is unusually large or oddly shaped. Our skills for driving a car would not be completely adequate in a huge truck, and so we would have to motor plan until we got used to the unfamiliar size, steering, and pedals of the truck.

Since motor planning is the first step in learning skills, the dyspraxic child usually has a shortage of skills. He has to motor plan each task over and over again. He does manage to acquire some specific "splinter skills" without gaining the generalized ability to organize his actions. (See Chapter 4 for a discussion of splinter skills.) Once the dyspraxic child does learn a skill, he usually performs it quite well, as long as the situation is familiar.

Motor Planning

Postural reactions, centrally programmed movements, and learned motor skills do not take much attention or volition; it is enough merely to have a general goal in mind. Motor planning, on the other hand, requires attention. Attention enables the brain to plan the kind of messages to send to the muscles and the sequence in which to send them.

An infant motor plans picking up a rattle, putting a spoon into his mouth, and crawling through a doorway—until these become skills and no longer require planning. The young child motor plans putting on clothes, writing the alphabet, and speaking complete sentences. Learning to use a new tool—even a crayon or a knife—requires motor planning. An adult motor plans when he ties an unfamiliar knot, does a new dance step, or learns a new job at work. For most men, sewing requires motor planning; for most women, using carpentry tools does.

 Motor planning is, in some ways, the highest and most complex form of function in children. Because it involves conscious attention, it is closely linked to mental and intellectual functions. It depends upon very complex sensory integration throughout the brain stem and cerebral hemispheres. The brain tells the muscles what to do, but the sensations from the body enable the brain to do the telling. Motor planning is the "bridge" between the sensory-motor and intellectual aspects of brain function.

Watch a child play a new game of hopscotch or climb an unfamiliar tree. He pays attention to every movement, and cannot pay attention to anything else. If something takes his attention away from what he is doing, he has to stop moving because his attention cannot be on two different things at the same time. However, if his brain is well organized, he has to motor plan that task only a few times to master it. He learns quickly and soon can play that game or climb that tree spontaneously. He no longer needs to pay close attention to his movements and can now talk to his friends as he hops, and climb without deliberate caution.

Here are some examples of poor motor planning. I told a child to lie down on a bench. She put her shoulders down on the bench and then asked, "What do I do with my legs?" The problem here was that the sensations from her legs did not "tell" her what to do. A young woman, when asked to get up onto a table, had to step up onto a chair and then stand on the table before she could lie down. Although she was able to lie down on her bed at home without first standing on it, she could not do the same thing with the table. She had learned to lie down on her bed as a splinter skill, but this did not carry over to the slightly different task of lying on the table.

I was talking to a child while nearby another child was busy hitting a hanging ball with a cardboard tube that she held with both hands. The latter child had just acquired the ability to use both hands together.

She spoke sharply, "Be quiet! I'm doing this!" She had to concentrate so hard on motor planning the action of her hands that she could not cope with the sounds of nearby conversation. Her request was, of course, honored.

The Body Percept and Motor Planning

Both motor planning and motor skills require a perception of how the body is designed and functions as a mechanical unit. Sensory input from the body must be organized into a clear-cut "picture" of the body. The brain refers to this internal sensory picture to move the body accurately. The sensory picture is stored in the nervous system, and so it may be called a *neuronal model*. It may also be called a *body image, body scheme*, or *body percept*. We shall use the latter term. To understand developmental dyspraxia, we must first discuss the way in which our body percept is formed and used in motor planning.

Neural Memories

In Chapter 3, we discussed the process by which sensory experience is stored in groups of neural interconnections. Every time a neural message passes through a synapse, the structure and chemistry of that synapse change, so it transmits that type of message more easily in the future. In other words, the repeated use of a synapse for a particular sensory-motor function creates a neural memory of that function.

A newborn infant has very few memories stored in his synapses. As he interacts with the world, his synapses gradually "fill up" with sensory-motor information. We have neural memories in our brain for everything we know: all words, every visualization, every face we recognize, every sequence of numbers we use, every motor skill. The body percept is a composite memory of every part of the body and all the movements those parts have performed.

Our body percept consists of "maps" of every part of our body, somewhat like a world atlas. As a child moves and does things, he stores countless bits of sensory information, just as world explorers map the lands they discover. The more variations of movement the child performs, the more accurate his body "maps" will be. The brain can refer to its body percept to plan movements, in much the same way as we use maps to navigate a journey. The more accurate the "maps," the more able one is to "navigate" unfamiliar body movements.

Our body percept contains neural memories about all parts of our bodies: their size, weight, and boundaries; their current position relative to the rest of the body; and all the movements they have ever made. It also contains neural memories related to the environment—information about the nature of gravity, the hardness of some things, the flexibility of others, and so on. Thus the brain is able to know how fast and how hard each muscle must work to accomplish a task, what to do and not to do with a tool, and whether we will fall if we move in a certain way.

We can compare our body percept to an "automobile percept." After we have driven a particular car for some time, we have a good "feeling" for the size of the car, the amount of steering needed to turn a corner, and how much to push the pedals to speed up or slow down. This knowledge comes from seeing and feeling how the car responds in every moment of driving. A good driver recalls this information so automatically that he never has to think about it. An inaccurate "automobile percept" is apt to lead to accidents, and the dyspraxic child has a lot of accidents because he has an inadequate body percept.

The Contribution of Touch Sensations to the
Body Percept and Motor Planning

Most children with minimal brain dysfunction show some irregularity in their tactile processes. Usually their sense of touch is not decreased, as it is when the dentist gives us a shot of Novocain. Sometimes, on the contrary, the child has a heightened sensitivity to touch sensations and experiences discomfort from ordinary tactile experiences. This type of disorder will be discussed in Chapter 7.

The most common tactile disorder lies in inaccurate localization of touch stimuli and inability to identify its meaning in relationship to space. In other words, the child has trouble discriminating and identifying things that touch him or that he touches. He knows when he is touched, but he cannot feel whether it was his middle finger or ring finger that was touched. He feels something in his hand, but he cannot tell whether it is a nickel or a button.

Why is poor tactile discrimination so common among children with sensory integrative dysfunction? Touch sensations come into the brain from every bit of skin surface and travel to almost every part of the brain. Disorder in almost any area of the brain is apt to interfere with tactile discrimination, although the problem is different in each child.

How Are Sensations Discriminated?

Sensations from the skin travel up the spinal cord to layers of the brain stem and cerebral hemispheres. A sensory picture is organized at each level, and each level sends this information to other levels. At each higher level, discrimination is more accurate and precise. Some of the "noise" or irrelevant information is taken out, and the "signal" is felt more clearly. A similar process occurs when we turn the dials on a radio to reduce static and make the sound clearer.

Only a small portion of the tactile input that enters our brain goes high enough in the cerebral hemispheres to reach our conscious awareness. We are usually not aware of a tactile stimulus unless we focus our attention on the part of the body that is being touched, or the stimulus is strong enough to draw our attention. Meanwhile countless other tactile sensations—from the pressure and movement of air and clothes and furniture against our bodies—keep our tactile system active. The fact that we are not aware of most tactile input does not mean that it is not important. Continuous tactile input is tremendously important in keeping the brain organized. If the brain is deprived of touch stimulation, it very quickly becomes disorganized. As we have described in Chapter 4, extreme disorganization has been found in rats deprived of handling, in infant monkeys deprived of maternal touch, in institutionalized human children, and in normal adults in sensory deprivation chambers.

Nonspecific and Specific Tactile Input

When neuroscientists study the tactile system, they find that much tactile input is "nonspecific"; it does not tell the brain where it came from on the skin, and it does not require a specific perceptual or motor response. This input instead helps to maintain a balance of excitatory and inhibitory forces throughout the nervous system. It "nourishes" the brain and helps to keep it operating smoothly.

On the other hand, some tactile input—particularly sensations from the hands, fingers, and mouth area—is very "specific." It goes to the highest level of the brain, the sensory cortex, which is divided into sections, one section for each part of the body. A very detailed picture is formed of these sensations in the sensory cortex, and the person can respond in a very precise way. Writing is a good example of an activity that involves many specific tactile sensations. The pencil touches exact spots on the fingers, and these stimuli are used by the brain to send out very precise information to the finger muscles that hold and move the pencil. Each bit of tactile information must travel to exactly the right spot in the sensory cortex, and the brain must send its response back very quickly to exactly the proper muscle. If the arm and hand have "gone to sleep," sensations from skin and muscles are so deficient that writing is very difficult.

But if the incoming information is vague, so also will be the outgoing directions. In that case, it would be like writing with a mitten on your hand; you would feel the pencil and the table, but the sensations would be diffuse and poorly defined. That is the way it is for the dyspraxic child. The tactile information is vague and results in a body percept that is not precise.

Here are some things you can do to get the feeling of what it might be like to have a touch system that doesn't give precise information. Take off your shoes, sit down, and put your feet on a chair so that your toes are not touching anything. Close your eyes and ask a friend to touch one of your three middle toes. Can you tell which toe was touched? Probably not very easily; but you can tell if the same test is done on your fingers. Most dyspraxic children have trouble identifying which finger was touched.

Now try to move just the toe that was touched. You will find this frustrating, because the human brain is not designed to direct isolated movement of the middle toes. The dyspraxic child feels a similar frustration when he tries to move a single finger.

Try wearing a pair of thick gloves while setting the table. See how you have to think about picking up the silverware because your limited sense of touch doesn't guide you in moving your hands.

Now try this. Cross your arms at the wrists with palms facing each other, interlace your fingers, and then bend your elbows to bring your hands almost under your chin. Ask another person to point to (but not touch) one of the six middle fingers. Try to move just that finger. Notice how hard you have to think to be able to move the correct finger. Now ask your friend to *touch* one of the fingers, and see how easily you know which finger to move. It is easy because the tactile information enables you to use your body percept of your hands, whereas without touch, you cannot tell from the unusual view of your fingers which movement to plan and execute.

How Proprioception Contributes to the Body Percept and Motor Planning

Proprioception from the muscles and joints also contributes to our body percept. Without that information, we would not know where the parts of our body are or how they are moving. During movement, proprioception updates our body percept so that the brain can plan the next movement correctly, and then contract the right muscles at the right time. Proprioception is often referred to as *kinesthesia*.

Imagine trying to drink a cup of hot coffee blindfolded. How do you know where your mouth is and how to get the cup there without spilling the coffee? How do you know how much effort to use in holding up the cup? If your muscles told you that it were filled with lead, you might use so much effort that the coffee would go flying.

You know these things, because the sensations from your muscles and joints tell your brain where your mouth is, where your hand is, how heavy the cup is, and how fast you are moving it. Without that information, you would have to use trial and error to get the cup from saucer to mouth, and it would be foolhardy to attempt such a feat with hot coffee. Then you would not open your mouth until the cup touched your face, since you would not know how close it was until it got there.

Try standing across the room from a light switch. Look at the switch and then close your eyes, walk across the room, and turn the switch on. This time you need to integrate proprioceptive sensations with vestibular input to motor plan without visual aid. You probably won't hit the switch exactly, but you will know about how far to walk, when to put your hand out, how high to reach, and when to slow down so that you don't bump into the wall.

We are usually not aware of proprioception unless we think about it; however, if it were not there, we would have a terrible time doing things. How many times have you closed a cupboard door without even looking at it? You were guided by proprioceptive signals and your neural memories of previous proprioceptive experience. Life would be much harder if we had to look at everything before moving.

Many children with minimal brain dysfunction have a reduced sense of proprioception, but most of them have a little. The sense is often vague and hazy, and they rely upon vision more than normal children. If they cannot see, they are lost. They hardly know where their hands and feet are. They cannot sense how much muscular effort they need to accomplish something, and so they often break their toys. They stumble over things and have frequent accidents.

To test the sense of kinesthesia, or joint position and movement, the therapist uses a piece of paper with points labeled "your house," "John's house," "Mary's house," and so on. She holds a piece of cardboard in front of the child's eyes so that he cannot see his hands, and places his finger on "your house." She then takes his finger to "John's house" and gives him some time to process the proprioceptive information about where his hand is. Then she brings his finger "back home" and asks him to go to "John's house" by himself. If the child has not processed proprioception adequately, he will probably place his finger far from the correct point on many of these trips. By comparing his accuracy with the performances of other children, the therapist can determine how well the child processes muscle and joint sensory information.

Sometimes, when the therapist moves the child's hand, she feels that his arm moves lightly and easily with her. However, if the child has trouble processing muscle and joint sensations, his arm feels heavy and hard to pull along. This child will feel heavy like a sack of potatoes in other situations too. It is hard to help him get onto a piece of equipment or move through an obstacle course or climb a jungle gym. On a scooter board, he may lie with half his body off the scooter without even knowing it.

The Vestibular System's Contribution to the Body Percept and Motor Planning

The sensations of gravity and movement are intermingled with muscle, joint, and skin information to complete the body percept. Vestibular information orients our body "maps" to the space around us. It is not enough for a map maker to survey the land; he must also relate this information to the magnetic poles. "Maps" of the muscles and joints and skin would be useless without "maps" of the gravitational field that acts upon the body. Vestibular information is especially important in "navigating" movements of the entire body.

The vestibular nuclei send impulses down the spinal cord to modulate the processing of muscle, joint, and skin information. If the vestibular system does not modulate the other senses, they are less efficient. Children with vestibular problems usually have some deficiencies in proprioceptive and tactile processing. To improve their motor planning, these children need activities involving a lot of vestibular, tactile, and proprioceptive stimulation along with adaptive responses that help organize these sensations.

The impulses from the vestibular system generate the muscle tone that keeps the muscles firm and ready to respond. Most children with minimal brain dysfunction have low muscle tone, and this reduces the amount of proprioception the muscles send back into the nervous sytem. This is one more reason why we must develop the vestibular system to help the child motor plan.

Internal Feedback

The brain sends out a motor command that causes the muscles to move the body and do something to the environment. As the brain causes things to happen in the environment, these results produce sensory input that "feeds back" into the nervous system. This is *external feedback* and is often visible or audible; we see that we have pushed a book off a table and we hear it fall. However, there is also an *internal feedback* that we do not see or hear. Every time we actively send out a motor command, the brain monitors that command and uses it to interpret the sensory input that results from the movement. Internal feedback records in the brain the motor command before it is completely executed. This "before the fact" information is essential for developing the ability to motor plan. External feedback comes into the brain too late for the person to change the plan.

When the body is moved passively, the brain does not send out a motor command, and so there is no internal feedback. Therefore, in therapy, we want the dyspraxic child to direct his own movements. The more he moves himself, the more internal feedback he gives himself. Self-directed movement is one of the "keys" to developing better motor planning.

Doing without Thinking

Many people find that they don't have to think about what they are doing to do it well; instead they let their thoughts and efforts stop and simply allow their brain to do the work spontaneously. A cafe waitress balances plates and silverware on her hand without thinking about it. A beginner at dance tries to think about the steps, but can do the dance well only when he stops trying to understand it. A seamstress or housewife finds that her hands and fingers move "just right." The movement comes fairly automatically simply because the task is there to be done. Some people have called this process "going with the flow."

Thinking is a good way to decide what to do, but is not very useful in the action of doing. The anatomy and physiology of our muscles are far too complex and things happen much too fast. The information in our body percept is sensory rather than mental, and so this information is not always in our conscious minds. The well-functioning brain can process sensory input, relate this input to the body percept, and form a motor plan, all without deliberate thinking. Thinking may actually interfere with the spontaneous processing of sensory input and motor responses. However, this automatic ease and gracefulness can occur only through good sensory integration. A person may have lots of motor skills, but still be unable to "go with the flow" of sensory processing.

The dyspraxic child cannot "go with the flow." His body percept is so poorly organized that his hands and feet often go the wrong way, and everything gets confused. He tries as hard as he can, but his trying is ineffective. Parents and teachers see that he is having a hard time, and try to help him with instructions and explanations. Unfortunately, an intellectual approach cannot solve the child's sensory integrative problems. Words cannot organize the brain. Instead of telling the child to move his left foot or explaining what that foot is supposed to do, it is often better simply to touch the foot without saying a word. The sensations may tell him how to move.

Developmental Dyspraxia: What Is It?

Developmental dyspraxia is a brain dysfunction that hinders the organization of tactile, and sometimes vestibular and proprioceptive, sensations and interferes with the ability to motor plan. The word "developmental" indicates that the problem begins early in the child's life and affects his development as he grows.

We can't see poor sensory integration, but we can see poor motor coordination. Therefore, dyspraxia *appears* to be a motor problem, just as other types of sensory integrative disorders appear as academic learning problems. We cannot see the problem itself; we can see only its physical manifestation. In trying to help these children, it is important to remember that the problem is inside the child, in the way that his brain processes sensations.

Manifestations of Developmental Dyspraxia

The dyspraxic child is poor at motor planning, and so he often does too much motor planning on each task. When he tries to learn a game or a sport, he has to motor plan it over and over again, because it doesn't "sink in." He wants to learn, and he tries very hard, but his body percept doesn't tell him how to learn.

Most children, when confronted with a toy that involves manipulation, will know immediately what to do with it. If it is a barrel, they get inside and roll; if it is a jungle gym, they climb on it; if it is a set of blocks, they build a tower. Sometimes this is not what the manufacturer of the toy expected the child to do, but the child knows his own nervous system and he knows how to have fun.

The dyspraxic child, on the other hand, has less of a sense of his body and what it can do. He doesn't realize the opportunites for fun. He may get inside the barrel, but it doesn't occur to him to roll. Or he may simply think that the barrel is a trash can and ignore it. Instead of manipulating toys and creating opportunities for fun, he simply pushes them around, or lines them up in rows. Barrels, tricycles, jungle gyms, and other large toys may have very little meaning for him because his body percept is so poorly developed.

An intelligent dyspraxic child may see how other children are playing with a toy, and he may understand what they are doing, but still be unable to plan playing with that toy. Driven by the need to play with it, the child pulls or pushes too hard on it and frequently breaks it. His clumsiness makes him accident-prone and messy. Sometimes he deliberately destroys a toy in his effort to cope with his frustration and feelings of inferiority.

A child with a poorly developed body percept will have trouble putting on clothes and using the buttons and zippers. How can be fit clothes around his body if he doesn't even know how his body is designed? Tying shoelaces is particularly difficult.

A precise, clear body percept is also necessary in using tools, for a tool is actually an extension of the body. Crayons, felt-tip pens, and pencils are the most common tools, and it is a common complaint of teachers that the child has trouble learning to write. Unfortunately, the complaint is usually, "He is so messy; he must learn to be more neat." But the child cannot "learn to be neat" until he integrates the sensations from his body.

Parents are often confused by the ease with which the child sits and walks. They remember that he sat up at the same age as other babies, learned to walk according to schedule, and can now walk up to a chair and sit down without problems; so they expect him to dress himself and tie his shoes as well as any other child. But walking and sitting are based upon central programs, and the child's problem is not in central programming. Parents who do not understand that a praxis problem is something different often say, "He can do it if he really wants to, or if he tried hard enough." They do not realize how much effort goes into the doing.

Parents may also be confused when they see the child learning specific splinter skills. If a dyspraxic child is bright, he can learn a specific task like buttoning by practicing for a long time until his brain can form that particular motor message. But then he still lacks the generalized ability to motor plan, and so other tasks are just as difficult. Splinter skills are good to have, but they don't help the brain learn anything else.

A child once commented, "I can't do and think at the same time; I have to think first, then do." Having to think through every unfamiliar movement consumes a lot of energy. Without the spontaneous planning ability that comes from good sensory integration, a tremendous mental effort is required to figure things out. It just doesn't seem worthwhile to some dyspraxic children to spend all their energy doing something that everyone else can do easily.

The Effects of Dyspraxia on School Achievement

The fact that the brain is not doing one thing well suggests that it will not do a number of other things well. Many children with dyspraxia have learning problems, but not all of them do. It is possible to be dyspraxic and learn adequately, but it is much harder to learn. Being bright helps to compensate for the problem, but it does not necessarily make the child feel any better.

Early academic learning is dependent upon organizing a lot of sensory input, especially from the eyes and ears, but also from the vestibular, tactile, and proprioceptive receptors. As we shall see in Chapter 8, visual perception is somewhat dependent upon the sensations from the body and gravity. If these sensory systems are not working well, visual processing and reading may be more difficult.

A poorly organized body percept interferes with writing, coloring, and drawing. It also makes the child clumsy and confused on the playground. Other children may laugh at him and refuse to play with him. This often results in feelings of ineptness and powerlessness that carry over into the classroom.

A Checklist for Developmental Dyspraxia

Most of the symptoms of developmental dyspraxia are things the child does *not* do, rather than things he does do. The following is a list of some tasks and the ages by which almost all children have successfully motor planned those tasks. A normal child usually performs most of these tasks at ages earlier than those listed. If your child appears to think and reason all right, but has trouble learning many of these skills by the ages listed, he may be dyspraxic. It is important to take into account circumstances that may have given a particular child more or less opportunity to learn certain tasks.

Age	Task
6 months	Plays with rattles, blocks, string, etc., rather than merely grasping them, picking them up, or chewing on them.
1 year	Manipulates things, takes them apart, puts one thing inside another, rearranges them, makes noise by banging them together instead of merely pushing or pulling them around.
2 years	Feeds himself with a spoon. Holds a cup and drinks from it. Makes marks with a crayon.
3 years	Takes off and puts on a coat or dress. Uses a fork. Unwraps a stick of gum. Dries hands with a towel.
4 years	Buttons easy buttons. Fills glass from pitcher of water. Washes hands. Cuts with scissors. Climbs under, over, and into chairs, tables, boxes. Rides a tricycle. Jumps up with both feet together.
5 years	Puts on almost all clothes (except for tying shoe laces). Draws a cross with a crayon. Cleans himself at the toilet. Makes a tent or house out of furniture and blankets. Cuts and pastes creative paper designs.
6 years	Hops on one foot. Prints his name. Colors between the lines in a coloring book. Uses a pencil eraser. Plays catch with a ball.
7 years	Bathes himself with assistance. Uses hammer, screwdriver, and pliers, although not well. Spreads butter with a table knife. Ties shoelaces.
8 years	Writes his name in longhand. Pins two things together with a safety pin. Uses a straight pin, needle, paper clip, etc. Jumps rope.

Age	Task
9 years	Uses a table knife for cutting.
	Bathes himself without assistance.
	Uses a hammer, screwdriver, and pliers efficiently.
	Skips (girls usually learn earlier).
10 years	Beats an egg with a spoon without spilling it.
	Breaks an egg; separates the yolk from the white.
	Peels an apple with a knife.
	Imitates you as you fold paper to make a hat.

If your child has not learned to do many of the above things by the ages listed and also shows the following problems, he is probably dyspraxic.

1. Does things in an inefficient way.
2. Has low muscle tone, which makes him seem weak.
3. Needs more protection than other children—has trouble "growing up." His mother may have to be overprotective since he has such a hard time with life.
4. He is accident-prone. He has many little accidents, such as spilling milk, and big accidents, such as falling off his tricycle.
5. Is more emotionally sensitive to things that happen to him. His feelings are easily hurt. He cannot tolerate upsets in plans and expectations.
6. Complains more about minor physical injuries. Bruises, bumps, and cuts seem to hurt him more than they do other children.
7. Is apt to be stubborn or uncooperative. His nervous system is inflexible, so he wants things his way.

How Does It Feel to Be a Dyspraxic Child?

Difficulty in motor planning is not the only way in which dyspraxia manifests itself. Dyspraxic children often—but not always—have trouble coping with many life situations. The brain that cannot organize sensations from the body usually also has trouble organizing all the sensations that arise in situations where there are many people or things. The child cannot modulate all those sensations and is easily overloaded. His nervous system may not be able to cope with the stresses that others can. In addition, his responses are so inadequate that he may have to do things twice and deal with the mess he caused the first time.

His body percept is so poorly developed that he has no clear sense of being a physical being. He has a real identity crisis. Since he has difficulty knowing who he is or what he is, he may be afraid to pretend or imagine. I once commented to an apraxic child that she looked like a princess, and she wailed, "I'm not a princess; I'm Pamela!" This tenuous hold on physical identity makes for a very insecure sense of emotional being. The child is in bondage to his own body. The disorder in his nervous system prevents normal personality development. He acts in an unlovable manner, yet he is a child who needs extra love and reassurance.

Most of us who can relate to physical objects in an effective manner do not begin to realize how terribly threatening motor demands can be to a child who cannot handle them or who has to struggle to handle them. It is very frustrating to imagine getting things done, but not being able to do them. It must be similar to wanting to feed oneself when both hands are in complete casts. The dyspraxic child feels somewhat impotent. Not only is his relationship to himself impaired, but he cannot have a normal relationship to his environment. He has very little control over his life and he often feels powerless or incompetent. He may try to compensate by controlling other children, or by trying to manipulate the situation. He sometimes tries to preserve the integrity of his self by being stubborn and uncooperative.

Dyspraxic children often think that their lack of control over the environment is due to someone else or the environment itself. They may say things like "The wall hit me," or "You're making the chair wobble." It's always someone else who caused the mistake. The pencil isn't right; the paper isn't right. In addition, some dyspraxic children experience gravitational insecurity; even the earth seems unfriendly.

Upon this impotent, insecure, bewildered child, adults often impose themselves, usually with good intentions. Adults gear their demands to the child's intelligence level, rather than to his motor planning ability. When they see him do a few splinter skills or centrally programmed movements well, they demand that he do other things just as well. Ignoring the fragility of his emotions, they expect him to cope with more stress and confusion than his nervous system can handle.

The dyspraxic child is not neurologically equipped to buffer threats to his selfhood. Even the slightest problem, such as breaking a pencil, may lead to a catastrophic reaction. If he musters up the courage to try a task and experiences any difficulty at all, he may never try that task again. The child's feelings of insecurity increase whenever he notices that other children are successful with some task at which he fails. It is no wonder that dyspraxic children often become negative, resistive, and manipulative.

He may be emotionally labile—happy one minute, crying the next. A dyspraxic child may try to remain a baby and deal with situations only in a baby-like manner. He does not have the neurologic competence to "act his age" in dealing with things. This child needs parental support and reassurance for more years than most children. He needs adults to see his world the way he sees it.

Often the best approach with dyspraxic children is to avoid exposing them to external pressure or failure. Let the child's own inner drive give him direction as long as this is in some way constructive. Let him develop at his own pace, since he cannot develop at someone else's pace. Let him avoid tasks that threaten him. Give him understanding, protection, and opportunity at his own level. But, above all, give him sensory integrative therapy to help his brain function more efficiently.

CHAPTER 7

TACTILE DEFENSIVENESS

Tactile defensiveness is a subtle, yet serious neural disorder. It is frequently seen in children with learning disabilities, minimal brain dysfunction, and more serious conditions. The tactilely defensive child is usually hyperactive and distractible, and this is the aspect that bothers parents and teachers the most. However, not all hyperactive and distractible children are this way because of poor tactile sensory processing.

The neural disorder that causes a child to be tactilely defensive does not necessarily hinder learning, but the discomfort and behavioral reactions caused by this disorder do interfere with the learning process. Very often the child is emotionally insecure. Apparently the disorder in the tactile system also makes the emotions easily upset. Tactile defensiveness is the child's way of experiencing and reacting to touch sensations, but these experiences and reactions reflect a more serious condition inside his nervous system.

The Symptoms

Tactile defensiveness is the tendency to react negatively and emotionally to touch sensations. The reaction occurs only under certain conditions. Most of us react negatively to tactile stimuli that are particularly offensive, such as a bug crawling on our skin or a hand touching us by surprise. For the tactilely defensive child, many more touch sensations cause these reactions. He is overly sensitive to stimuli that other people would hardly feel. Touch sensations cause major disruptions in his nervous system and cause negative emotions and behaviors.

Inhibition is the neural process in which one part of the nervous system prevents another part from overreacting to sensory input. Tactile sensations from clothes touching the body and sensations from the skin itself are constantly entering everyone's nervous system. However, most of us inhibit our perception of these sensations and prevent our nervous system from responding to them. The tactilely defensive child does not have enough of this inhibitory activity, and so these sensations—and many others—make him feel uncomfortable and want to move about a lot. It is very difficult to pay attention in school when your skin or your clothes do not feel comfortable and you have to fidget to reduce the discomfort.

The child may prefer a long-sleeved shirt or blouse to keep his arms covered, or he may want to keep a sweater on even when he is warm. He may avoid getting his hands in paste or finger paint, or he may not want to walk barefoot in grass or sand. He may not like to have someone bathe him or he may not like to go wading because splashes of water may overactivate his nervous system. Certain fabrics, such as wool, some synthetics, or rough-textured material, may cause discomfort.

When he feels particularly secure, especially with someone he loves, he may want the extra touch of cuddling. At other times, he may avoid even his mother's touch. The tactilely defensive child is in quite a quandary; he needs more touch than other children, but he is less able to modulate tactile impulses and use them to keep his nervous system balanced. Parents of tactilely defensive children need to be particularly observant and understanding. Love alone is not sufficient to relieve the problems of these children, but it does help. Therapy will help even more.

To add to the child's problems, his reactions to touching interfere with his social relationships. Relatives and friends may be offended when he shrugs off their hugs and kisses; they may assume that he dislikes them, when actually his rejection is not personal. The friendly relative who wants to show affection by rubbing his hand back and forth through the child's hair may offend the child's tactile system. Even a friendly arm around the shoulders may feel uncomfortable. Tickling may be extremely uncomfortable for a tactilely defensive child. Even though he appears to laugh, he may be miserable and want to strike out at the person tickling him.

The child has trouble playing with other children, because they do not realize when they are causing him discomfort. Games like tag may bring him agony. The child reacts not only to actual touch, but also to the fear that someone might touch him. Being touched from behind or when one cannot anticipate the touch is especially threatening, and so making the tactilely defensive child wait in line with other children is just inviting an incident. His teacher then considers the problem to be "poor behavior" and does not notice that the child has a physical reason for behaving the way he does.

Sometimes the child with tactile defensiveness avoids many objects that other children like, such as fuzzy stuffed toys, but other tactilely defensive children seek an extra amount of comfortable tactile stimulation. The tactile input that feels good is organizing to the nervous system and helps reduce the negative reaction. So some tactilely defensive children have a special need for a "security blanket" or a teddy bear. They may like to roll up in a blanket while watching television or lie on a carpet with thick pile.

Do not try to get a tactilely defensive child to overcome his negative reactions by telling him that he does not need to act that way. To deny that he has a real problem will not make it go away and will only make him feel guilty. The discomfort is real and the child cannot prevent himself from reacting to it.

The Child's Experience

Imagine yourself lying on a sunny beach; your eyes are closed and you feel the warm sun shining on your bare feet. Suddenly someone runs a stick quickly, but lightly up the sole of your foot. Even though your nervous system was in a very relaxed state, that tactile stimulus would probably make you angry or alarmed, even though it was not painful. Your reaction would be less if the person pressed the stick slowly and firmly on your skin. This is because quick, light touch sensations tend to arouse the nervous system more than firm, nonmoving pressure sensations. It does not take an intense sensation to cause a negative reaction, and this is particularly true for the tactilely defensive child.

The child with this neural disorder actually experiences touch stimuli differently from other people. Something that feels fine to other children may be irritating to this child. Sometimes he can tell us what he feels. Some say that the touch of a pencil feels like a needle, or an electric shock, or an insect biting. Often touch feels like being tickled, and this is not pleasurable, although it may cause a reflex giggle. More often, the tactilely defensive child is not fully conscious of what he feels other than that another person is making him angry or uncomfortable. The poor tactile processing usually occurs in the brain stem or in subconscious areas of the cerebral hemispheres, and so the child does not realize that he is reacting to touch sensations. The child with good self-control is apt to find socially acceptable excuses for avoiding what he is doing. When his brain needs to escape from touch sensations, he may say, "I want a drink of water," or "I have to go to the bathroom," or "My mother doesn't want me to do that."

Meanwhile, he is often miserable, and his misery leads to behavior that makes other people miserable.

What Is Going on in the Nervous System?

To the tactilely defensive child a simple touch on the arm may be a primal threat, just as it would be to an animal that is not tame. The natural reaction to a primal threat is a primal response such as anger, fighting, or running away.

Touch, smell, and sound are the senses most animals have used to detect environmental danger. As the brain evolved to survive in nature, it formed a set of neural reactions to sensations that indicated that danger was nearby. These neural reactions aroused attention and prepared the nervous system and muscles to fight or flee. A few thousand years of living in civilized society have not changed the basic neural patterns that evolved over millions of years. Thus human beings automatically react to danger by either running away or fighting back.

However, as the human brain evolved, mechanisms formed to inhibit the fight-or-flight responses in favor of newer processes for perceiving the shapes and textures of things touching the skin. Part of the brain inhibited the protective reaction and enabled the individual to remain calm and focus his attention on the meaning of the touch stimulus.

So there are two types or "modes" of response to tactile stimuli; one is called "defensive," or "protective," because it evolved to protect animals from danger, and the other is known as "discriminative"; it was described in the preceding chapter. Defensive processes are simple automatic reactions; discriminative processes involve complex refinement in the cerebral hemispheres. The normal person automatically uses whichever mode he needs at each moment. When we touch a hot stove or an insect bites us, our defensive mode takes over. When we need to feel the difference between a penny and a dime in our pocket, or between cotton and wool, we rely upon our discriminative mode.

The stimulus at the skin helps to determine whether the defensive or discriminative mode will control our response. Pain sensations activate the defensive system, while deep pressure sensations tend to modulate or inhibit that system. So when you strike your shin against something, you rub the skin to lessen the pain. Rubbing produces tactile impulses that inhibit or block the flow of pain impulses. Pressure sensations tend to balance out excess activity in the protective system. We scratch a mosquito bite because the deep pressure stimuli prevent the tactile system from conducting itch sensations; and so the itch disappears as long as we scratch, but reappears when we stop. Treatment for tactile defensiveness is based on the same principle; sensations of firm, deep pressure will help to modulate the tactile processes that have been causing distress.

The brain uses other sensations, particularly vestibular and proprioceptive sensations, to balance the tactile sensory flow between the protective and discriminative modes. In addition, the tactile sensations from all parts of the body help to balance the flow of each particular tactile input. Therefore when vestibular and tactile and proprioceptive sensations from the entire body are not integrated, the two modes of response to tactile stimuli are not well balanced. The tactilely defensive child has too much protective activity and not enough discriminative processing. Instead of finding out what sensations mean, he tends to react to them in a fight-or-flight way.

The face has a large number of tactile receptors and is very important for survival. Animals evolved tendencies to be especially protective about their faces, and therefore the tactilely defensive child is particularly defensive about his face, especially around his mouth. This poses quite a problem when the child must have dental work. Even washing his face may be an ordeal for both parent and child. A certain amount of evasive reaction may be natural in children under three years, but if an older child moves his face away from a wash cloth, his nervous system may be imbalanced toward the defensive mode.

Many tactilely defensive children cannot tolerate having their hair washed or cut. The tactile system serving the head and face is anatomically different from the system for the rest of the body, and so the defensiveness

around the head may be more severe than that of the rest of the body.
When the barber lightly touches the child's hair and scalp, he is stimulating the child with exactly the type of sensations that are most apt to
over-arouse the defensive system. This may make the child move around so
much that the barber will have great difficulty doing his job and maintaining his patience. Pity the child, not the barber, for the child is suffer-
ing much more—and his problems do not end when he leaves the chair.
Parents can sometimes make hair washing or cutting less uncomfortable
by massaging the child's scalp beforehand. The pressure sensations may
have a modulating effect that will last during the cutting or washing.

The brain interprets touch sensations initiated by the person himself
differently from sensations from someone else's touch. There is nothing
to be protective about when we touch ourselves. Other people can tickle
you; you can't tickle yourself. A tactilely defensive child may enjoy touching himself with a feather, but feel uncomfortable if someone else touches
him with the same feather. He usually feels most comfortable with his
mother's touch, and most uncomfortable when a stranger touches him.
For therapy to be effective, the child must trust the therapist enough to
allow her to touch him.

In therapy, we cover equipment with carpet so that the child stimulates
his own tactile receptors as he moves over the equipment. Since these
tactile sensations come from his own body actions, his nervous system
can usually integrate them. Tactile defensiveness interferes with the child's
inner drive, but that drive is still within the child. If we let him follow
that inner drive in stimulating himself, he will usually do what is best for
his nervous system.

Therapists also use direct tactile stimulation with a brush to reduce
defensive tactile processes, but only when the child is able to modulate
and integrate that input. Vestibular stimulation also helps to modulate
the tactile system. Brushing is sometimes given after vestibular stimulation, for the two types of sensations tend to modulate each other.

What Has Gone Wrong?

As with the other sensory integrative dysfunctions, we never know
exactly why the child has his problem. We usually cannot even guess what
caused the problem and when it began. In some cases of tactile defensiveness, we suspect that inadequate oxygen during birth predisposes the
brain toward a tactile imbalance. The nuclei that process tactile sensations are very vulnerable at that time of life. As described in Chapter 4,
Dr. William F. Windle found that some of these nuclei were damaged
when monkeys were asphyxiated at birth.

We also know that a lack of adequate tactile stimulation increases
tactile defensiveness. When animals are not touched and handled during
infancy, they fail to develop the ability to cope with stress. The monkeys
that Harlow raised without comfortable touch experiences grew up to be
hostile and violent; they would not let humans or other monkeys play
with them. When normal healthy adults are deprived of sensory experi-

ences for even a few hours, they become overly excitable and distractible for some time after they return to a normal environment.

Very few of the children with sensory integrative dysfunctions have actually been deprived of the touching and handling needed for tactile development. Instead, it appears that they were not able to integrate the sensations they did receive. They were hugged and caressed about as much as other children, but these experiences were not sufficient to make the brain develop well.

A Checklist for Tactile Defensive Behaviors

If your child frequently or consistently shows several of the following reactions, he is showing tactile defensive behavior. If several of these behaviors are seen in conjunction with hyperactivity and the inability to focus on a task, it is probable that he is tactilely defensive and should receive help from a sensory integration therapist.

1. Avoids being touched on the face. He may move his head away from things that are near his face. Washing his face may be especially difficult.
2. Finds the touching during dental work especially annoying and moves about a lot in the chair.
3. Is very distressed about having his hair cut or washed.
4. Dislikes it when people touch him, even in a friendly or affectionate way. Pulls away from a hug or even a pat on the shoulder. At other times, or from other people, he may accept the same kind of touch.
5. Touching the child while dressing him may elicit a negative reaction. Simply pulling up his sock may make him react.
6. Does not like it when someone bathes him or cuts his fingernails.
7. Tends to avoid physical contact with friends, even though he likes to talk to them and relate without touch.
8. Being approached from behind is more threatening than it is for other children.
9. Having people near him, even without touching, may cause him distress.
10. Often prefers long-sleeved shirt or blouse and wears a sweater or jacket even when he is warm.
11. Has unusual needs for touching or avoiding touching certain surfaces or textures, such as blankets, carpets, or stuffed toys.
12. Is sensitive to certain fabrics and avoids wearing clothes made of them.
13. Does not like to get his hands in sand, finger paint, paste, or similar materials.
14. Avoids going barefoot, especially in sand or grass.
15. When he was an infant, experienced great discomfort when his nose or ears were cleaned with a cotton swab.

Related Behavior Disorders

Although the negative reactions of children with poor sensory integration are most often to tactile stimuli, similar behaviors sometimes occur in reaction to odors or sounds. If the brain cannot inhibit the sensory input from the nose or ears, these sensations will bother the child and cause disruptive behaviors. The odors of food, perfume, furniture polish, or other chemicals may smell too strong. The noises of a fire truck, music, or other children may sound too loud. Careful observation is needed to notice when the child is reacting to these sensations rather than to something else that is happening at the same time.

REFERENCE

Ayres, A. Jean. Tactile functions: Their relation to hyperactive and perceptual motor behavior. *American Journal of Occupational Therapy*, 1964, *18*, 6-11.

CHAPTER 8

VISUAL PERCEPTION
AND AUDITORY-LANGUAGE DISORDERS

Until a few decades ago, disorders in visual perception, auditory processing, and language were the main areas investigated in individuals with brain dysfunctions. They are still among the major areas of concern to educators. Visual perception tests have fallen out of favor with many professionals because these tests do not always detect and rarely clarify learning problems. A different kind of test of visual processing is needed. The test of nystagmus is a better kind of test. When a school thinks that a child does not have good visual perception, they give paper and pencil work and table-top puzzle-type activities. This approach has promoted skills that enable children to succeed in some visual perception tasks, although they may lack the general ability to use their visual system efficiently for reading.

Education today is not designed to promote the development of sensory processing, which is the foundation for reading and computation; education assumes that the child has developed the sensory foundations and is ready to learn academics or at least visual perception tasks. So when society places pressure on schools to do a better job of teaching children to read, the schools respond by attempting to teach it to younger and younger children.

In some children, the brain is ready to read in kindergarten, but in others, the ability to visually process the printed word into spoken language has not developed adequately. For these children, sitting at a desk deprives them of the vestibular, proprioceptive, and tactile experiences they need to promote that development. The postponing of reading instruction until sensory integrative therapy has helped the child to improve his visual processing may help him to learn to read more quickly and better in the long run. It will also preserve his self-concept.

Visual and auditory processes are important, and the development of good language skills is a major objective of both education and therapy. Vision, hearing, and speech are central to being a competent social being. Why, then, does the sensory integration therapist apparently pay so little attention to these functions? Because she considers them to be the end products of many more fundamental aspects of brain function. Most of the children with learning disorders need to develop the vestibular, proprioceptive, and tactile functions of their brains. While the therapist appears to pay no attention to visual or auditory processes, she is actually trying to build the sensory-motor foundation for those processes.

Visual Perception Problems

Space and Form Perception

Most of us have forgotten what it was like to see as an infant. At birth we did not see things in the meaningful images we see now. We very quickly learned to recognize our mother's face because her presence meant that food and comfort were near. Later on, we moved about in our environment and thereby learned the physical nature of space and objects. This physical sensory-motor knowledge was gradually integrated with visual information to give us visual space and form perception.

Even before we could see at all, we had some sense of the space defined by gravity. In the womb, the input to our gravity receptors told us which way was up and which way was down. Our mother's movements stimulated our movement receptors to give us a sense of direction and speed. Thus our fetal brain began to "map out" the world outside the womb. The muscle and joint receptors were ready to give information to the brain, but the close quarters in the womb prevented most of the movements that produce muscle and joint sensations. Starting with birth, we learned to deal with much more space around our bodies in which we could move, see, and hear many more things.

All of our physical actions occur in relation to the space we occupy. Our abilities to comprehend the dimensions of space and the relationship of our body to space are processes that we had to learn. If a child has not learned to recognize how much space there is around him and how to orient himself to that space, he will have a hard time interacting with his physical environment. His difficulty may be most obvious in the way he colors with a crayon, writes with a pencil, follows a line of print, throws a ball, or keeps his room at home. When he has problems standing in line with other children or playing games, it may be harder to notice that poor spatial perception is causing those problems.

The things we see do not make good sense unless our brain knows where the earth is, and whether the head and body are in motion. The brain must hold the eyes and head steady so that we get a clear picture of the environment. Also, the brain must be able to direct the eyes in following the movements of objects and people. Any disorder in the processing of vestibular or eye and neck sensations will probably upset visual perception.

Self-Determined Movements

We learn to perceive space and relate ourselves to that space through adaptive responses and the resulting sensory inputs. Drs. Richard Held and Alan Hein did some interesting experiments that illustrate how important adaptive responses are to the development of visual perception.

One experiment was done with newborn kittens who were placed on an apparatus in an enclosure. Some of the kittens walked and pulled the apparatus around the enclosure with them, while the other kittens rode passively. Both groups of kittens had the same visual experience in seeing the walls of the enclosure. The kittens who were carried passively by the others did develop sight, but they could not use their sight to guide their movements effectively. They could not place their paws properly or move away from a place where they could fall, and they would blink at an approaching object. The kittens that actively moved to pull the apparatus developed normally without these problems. Passive movement and sight are not good enough; the individual must determine his own movements to integrate visual and motor processes. When the kittens were released from the apparatus, the ones that had been passively carried began to move about normally, and then quickly developed the functions they needed.

Held and Hein also experimented with people wearing prism glasses that made everything appear upside-down. After some time the brain could adapt to this upside-down visual input so that things seemed right side up again. However, the people wearing these prism glasses could make this adaptation only if they were able to move about actively and relate what they saw to what they touched and felt from movement.

Adaptation through Evolution

For millions of years, animals have moved themselves in relation to space and the forms in nature. Visual perception evolved through the adaptive responses that were critical to survival in those natural environments. Survival involved finding or catching a meal and avoiding being a meal for another animal.

For the first vertebrates, the fish and amphibians, visual perception was no more than the ability to see things that moved in very specific ways. A frog can see only things that move like flies or like animals that eat frogs; a hungry frog will ignore food that is stationary, but he will try to catch any small dangling object. This was the most advanced type of visual perception for millions of years, since there was no need to see small details in stationary objects; puzzle pieces and the alphabet had not yet been invented.

Next the capacity for spatial perception evolved so that reptiles could move about effectively. In fish, amphibians, and reptiles, visual input is processed almost entirely in the brain stem, since these animals have very small cerebral hemispheres. When a lizard moves, a part of its brain stem records an image of everything it sees. This information is used so that the lizard can find its way quite well. It does not bump into things; it can run away from a predator and find a good hiding place.

Early mammals lived in the trees where they had to see many things in all directions. Tree-living caused the visual system to take on a major role in the development of the brain. Primates, such as monkeys and apes and humans, have evolved a higher level of visual processing involving the fovea (the center of the eyeball) and the cerebral cortex. The fovea contains special receptor cells that can isolate small segments of the visual field and distinguish small details in a stationary object. The cerebral cortex processes these intricate visual details; but first the brain stem and lower levels of the cerebral hemispheres must organize the overall sensory picture.

In evolution, hundreds of millions of years of full body movements and vestibular, tactile, and proprioceptive integration paved the way for the development of neural processes that could analyze small details and symbolic meanings. The neural mechanisms for perceiving details and symbols evolved, "on top of" the older, more fundamental processes, just as a house is built upon a foundation. A house will stand if the roof is shaky, but it falls apart if the foundation is not secure. Sensory integration therapy is a natural approach; we roughly follow the same way that nature took during the evolution of vertebrates. We build the sensory-motor foundation first, and then work with the higher levels of brain function, because that is how brains are designed to develop.

The Dual Modes of Visual Perception

There are two major levels of brain activity in which human beings process visual input: the brain stem and the cerebral hemispheres. In the brain stem mode, vestibular input, proprioception from the eyes, neck, and body, and visual input are unified into one composite sensory process. The sensations from the neck muscles holding up the head are particularly important for this process. Vestibular, proprioceptive, and visual information are integrated to form a "map" that is used to "navigate" the body successfully in space. Without this map, a person has a hard time running without bumping into things, throwing a ball to a friend, or drawing a straight line on paper

After the vestibular, proprioceptive, and visual sensations are unified in the brain stem, they travel to several parts of the cerebral hemispheres for more specialized processing. These cerebral processes enable us to see a small area in great detail and in relationship to its background. They also help us direct our eyes when we voluntarily look at things. The muscles around the eyes aim the fovea "just right" to spot the details in the letters of the alphabet. If vestibular and proprioceptive sensations are not properly organized to keep the eyes moving smoothly, the child may suffer great discomfort when reading a book, similar to the discomfort we feel as we read movie titles when the film is flickering slightly.

If the visual area of the cerebral cortex is not in good communication with the vestibular system and the muscles, joints, and skin, visual discrimination will be poor. Thus children who do not receive precise information from their bodies also often have trouble with visual perception. Children whose major problem is in processing vestibular input usually, but not always, score low in visual perception tests.

The important thing about having two modes of visual processing is to have them work together and interact with each other. The following is a good example of how the brain stem and cerebral modes interact. Therapy involves many similar instances of sensory interaction.

A child walks toward a slide in the playground. He has an image of the slide in his visual cortex. The meaning of this image comes from both brain stem and cerebral processes. For him to stand in front of the ladder in the proper position to begin climbing, his brain stem must organize vestibular, proprioceptive, and visual information. The child knows he can safely climb the ladder, because he has climbed objects before and can relate the visual image of the ladder to its physical structure and his own sensory-motor abilities. He climbs to the top without being disoriented, because his brain stem helps him know where he is in space. The unification of visual, proprioceptive, and vestibular information helps him direct his body into a sitting position at the top of the slide. He slides down and gets pleasure from the vestibular stimulation.

A child with poor sensory integration may not want to play on a slide, because his nervous system has difficulty with some or all of these tasks. He may not be able to tell how high the slide is and he may be frightened of climbing that far away from the ground. He may not manage his body well on the ladder, because his proprioceptive sensations are disorganized. The tiny platform on the top of the slide may be a dangerous place if he has poor postural and equilibrium responses. To a child with gravitational insecurity, coming down even a very slow slide may make him feel as though he is sliding off the earth. If his vestibular system is underreactive, he may want to slide down over and over again, because his brain can never get enough vestibular stimulation.

Therapy for children with visual perception problems must involve both the brain stem and cerebral modes acting together in response to vestibular, proprioceptive, and visual stimulation. The neck muscles receive special emphasis, because sensations from them make a vital contribution to visual perception. When a child is lying on his stomach and he is holding his head up against gravity, the muscle contractions generate a lot of proprioceptive input, which then goes to the brain stem to help process the visual input. While in this position, the gravity receptors receive different stimulation, and when the child moves, other vestibular sensations are added for even more help in perceiving what is seen. For this reason, many activities in therapy place the child on his stomach while he moves.

All of the therapeutic activities that stimulate the receptors in the inner ears, muscles, joints, and skin may help in visual development. Improvement is most likely to occur if the dysfunction is in the brain stem. When the basic sensory systems are able effectively to support the higher levels of brain function, then it may be appropriate to use puzzles and paper and pencil work to promote visual perception. If therapy has helped the child organize his sensory systems, and he still has a visual problem, he may need to go to an optometrist who specializes in helping the eye muscles to work better.

A Checklist for Visual Perception Disorders

If your child shows one or more of these symptoms, he may have a deficit in visual sensory processing.

1. Does not build well with blocks as a young child.

2. Cannot put puzzles together as well as other children.
3. Is hesitant in going up or down curbs or steps.
4. Has trouble finding his way from one place to another and gets lost easily.
5. Does not like to be in strange places, because he knows he can easily become lost.
6. Does not draw well with a crayon or pencil as early as other children.
7. Has trouble recognizing the similarities and differences in patterns or designs.
8. Has a hard time seeing a particular figure against a confusing background.
9. Cannot make his letters stay between the lines or in the proper spaces for words.

Auditory and Language Problems

The sensory systems develop interdependently. The auditory system works closely with the vestibular system. In Chapter 5 we referred to the study of Stilwell, Crowe, and McCallum in which they found that many children with speech and language problems also showed shortened duration postrotary nystagmus. There are less obvious, but important connections to the touch and proprioceptive systems. When several sensory systems are involved in a problem, the auditory system is often the one in which the disorder is more evident. Thus it is inevitable that sensory integration therapists are equally concerned with some auditory and language problems, even though speech pathologists and audiologists specialize in this field.

The brain tends to operate as a whole in which each part interacts with many other parts. For the part of the brain that handles language and speech to function well, it is particularly important that it have good connections with the rest of an efficiently functioning brain, especially with the sensory and motor sections. Good whole brain processes enable the child to motor plan easily and efficiently. Talking, and in particular learning to talk, requires very complex motor planning. It requires the ability to initiate a motor act on one's own inner command. Then one must arrange the sequence of movements to make the sounds form a word. In one's brain one must decide which word follows which. Specific movements of the mouth, tongue, and lips are needed for good articulation.

These requirements are essentially the same as those involved in planning an action of the entire body. It is understandable that the child with a speech or language problem very often also has developmental dyspraxia. If there is special articulation difficulty, the problem may be oral apraxia. It is also logical that the therapy that helps the dyspraxic child to gain better sensory integration and motor planning also usually helps speech develop. It helps the processing of auditory input, and it helps in planning speech, because it helps the whole brain to function better. For specific training in language or speech, the child should get help from a speech specialist.

Since speech and language are one of the end products of sensory integration, they are often measured to judge the effectiveness of sensory integration therapy. Also, language comprehension is one of the easier aspects of behavior to measure—much easier than measuring emotionally based behavior or self-esteem, which are just as important as speech and language.

Levels of Auditory Processing

Just as there are several levels of visual processing, there are several levels of auditory processing. At the level of the brain stem, nuclei that are major processing centers for auditory input also associate that input with vestibular, proprioceptive, tactile, and vibratory input. Furthermore, the vestibular nuclei also receive auditory input and coordinate the two kinds of input. Brain stem processing is just as important for well-developed, discriminating hearing as it is for visual processing. As in visual functions, the brain stem processing provides the foundation for the more complex, higher level functioning that is necessary for language.

It is thought that sensory integrative therapy helps speech and language development by fostering the efficiency of the lower level processes. Increased vocalization is often seen when a child with a speech disorder receives the vestibular stimulation of therapy.

Studies of children with learning disorders due to auditory-language problems showed that their reading scores improved with sensory integration therapy focusing on vestibular, tactile, and proprioceptive stimulation and motor planning, but not including language training. The emphasis on brain stem sensory integration helped the cerebral hemispheres to cope with the language requirements of reading. The improved ability to motor plan and make adaptive responses also helped the higher level cognitive functions.

If a child fails to develop speech by two and one-half or three years of age, he should be checked by a therapist trained in sensory integration procedures. If the child's problem appears to especially involve brain stem processes, then therapy to help these processes is certainly the place to start aiding the child in his language development. Concurrent evaluation by a speech pathologist is also recommended.

REFERENCES

Ayres, A. Jean. Improving academic scores through sensory integration. *Journal of Learning Disabilities*, 1972, *5*, 336-343.

Held, Richard. Plasticity in sensory-motor systems. *Scientific American*, 1965, *213*, 84-94.

Held, Richard, & Hein, Alan. Movement-produced stimulation in the development of visually guided behavior. *Journal of Comparative and Physiological Psychology*, 1963, *56*, 872-876.

CHAPTER 9

THE AUTISTIC CHILD

Autism is a rare disorder of the brain that has puzzled professionals and parents since it was first recognized. The autistic child shows many of the symptoms of poor sensory processing that are seen in the child with minimal brain dysfunction, and his interactions with the physical environment are correspondingly poor. However, the autistic child has additional problems, both in the sensory-motor area and in other areas.

Autism is characterized by a lack of relating to other people, with the possible exception of one or two close individuals. The autistic child is most commonly described as being "in a world of his own," and he usually does not want others to intrude in that world. If he learns to speak, his speech is often limited; the articulation of words is usually all right, but the words lack intonation and sound monotonous and parrot-like. In addition, the autistic child has emotional problems. Sometimes he has too little emotion and hardly shows either love or fear. Some autistic children become very emotional, have tantrums, become extremely aggressive, and hurt other people.

Some sensory integration therapists have worked with autistic children, but in general, there is not as much professional experience in providing sensory integrative therapy for autistic children as there is with children having other types of brain dysfunction. Some young autistic children have profited from therapy, while others improve very slightly or not at all. It is encouraging to bring about *any* appreciable change in the brain organization of an autistic child, especially since biochemical approaches to the problem have offered only slight help, and behavior modification techniques merely control the child's behavior without changing the condition in his brain that causes that behavior.

The Sensory Processing Disorder

When autistic children are able to cooperate well enough to take the standard tests for sensory integrative function, their scores are usually similar to those of dyspraxic children. They have trouble localizing

123

tactile stimuli and knowing where their hands are if they cannot see them. They have a great deal of trouble motor planning, as shown in a test in which the examiner assumes an unusual posture and the child tries to imitate that posture. Although the child's postural responses are not really well developed, they are often better than those of some learning disabled children. This indicates that the child's brain stem is processing the proprioceptive and vestibular inputs needed for many postural responses. It also appears that the nerve tracts that carry information to the sensory areas of the cerebral cortex are doing an adequate job. Some other aspect of sensory processing is causing the problem; some other part of the brain is not working well.

There are three aspects of poor sensory processing that we see in autistic children. One, sensory input is not being "registered" correctly in the child's brain, and so he pays very little attention to most things, while at other times he overreacts. Two, he may not modulate sensory input well, especially vestibular and tactile sensations, and so he may be gravitationally insecure or tactilely defensive. Three, the part of his brain that makes him want to do things, especially new or different things, is not operating normally, and so the child has little or no interest in doing things that are purposeful or constructive.

The "Registration" of Sensory Information

Most of us have driven down a familiar street a number of times and then one day noticed something that we had never seen before. We might ask if the sign, or building, or whatever, is new and be surprised to find out that it had been there all the time. Our brains had just never before "decided" that that object was worth noticing. We are usually not even aware of why it attracted our attention when it did. Something might have been a little bit different about our image of the thing—perhaps the sun was striking it differently—and this slight difference caused our brain to "register" the image it had previously ignored.

There is a part of the brain (in the limbic system) that "decides" which sensory input is to be registered and brought to our attention, and also decides whether we will do something about that information. This part is not working well in the brain of the autistic child, and so he does not register many things that everyone else notices. The more poorly this part is working, the less the autistic child will respond to therapy.

Auditory and visual inputs are "ignored," or not registered, more often than the other types of sensory stimuli. The autistic child usually will not pay any attention to the sound of a bell, or to other noises, and will even fail to register what is said to him. Sometimes his brain will decide to record the input, and then the child does respond. Sometimes he seems to hear the sound as being louder than it is for others. Most people will stop registering a sound if it continues for a long time without much change. The autistic child does not grow accustomed to a continuous steady sound and "tune it out," and so he is apt to pay more attention to such sounds. Sometimes he over-registers one sound and under-registers another sound.

The autistic child also seems to ignore his visual environment. He stares through people, and avoids looking them in the eyes when they look at him. He often pays no attention to playthings, but sometimes his brain will decide to give the most careful and prolonged attention to some tiny detail, such as a spot on the floor. His brain has a hard time knowing which visual information is important and which is irrelevant. There is one kind of visual stimulus—moving stripes—that will attract the attention of most autistic children. The alternating colored and white stripes moving past the eyes activate "optokinetic nystagmus," which in turn stimulates the vestibular nuclei. (We have already discussed postrotary nystagmus, which consists of back and forth eye movements caused by vestibular stimulation. Optokinetic nystagmus is similar movements caused by visual input.) We believe that stimulation of the vestibular nuclei helps the brain to register the visual input and make it meaningful to the child.

The autistic child also has trouble registering other sensations. In one test, we apply a puff of air to the back of the neck; most people, including children with minimal brain dysfunction, will feel some discomfort in this and hunch their shoulders or turn to see what we are doing to them. Many autistic children show no response to this air puff test. Many of these children apparently do not register odors and have little sense of taste. They often do not react to falling or bumping themselves, as though they do not feel pain unless it is very intense. However, some autistic children are overly sensitive to the texture of things; when young, they may resist solid food because they do not like its texture. They may respond negatively to being touched by another person. Children with severe apraxia also sometimes have these sensory processing problems.

Very heavy touch-pressure is the kind of tactile stimulation that often produces a positive response in the autistic child. He may like to lie between two mats and have something heavy—like a large bolster—rolled over him. He may place his hands under very heavy things and enjoy pressure sensations that would hurt the average child. He wants to feel something, but perhaps only very strong sensations register in his brain. Some of these children act as though their hands felt uncomfortable much of the time, and the hard pressure made them feel better. Dyspraxic children also often like firm touch-pressure, but they seem to register the input more easily than the autistic child.

The autistic child senses input from his muscles and joints better than he does through his eyes and ears. Pulling the arms or legs stimulates the receptors in the joints and muscles, and autistic children often offer their arms and legs for the therapist to pull. We interpret this to mean that these sensations are satisfying. Again, it often seems that only very strong sensations—sensations strong enough to hurt others—are registered by the autistic brain.

Autistic children either seek movement and vestibular stimulation strenuously or reject it entirely. Neither response is normal. Some autistic children want great quantities of movement and seem to derive a lot of pleasure from this. Movements such as spinning and swinging do not make them dizzy or sick. This suggests that their brains do not register vestibular input as they should.

Almost all autistic children show a short duration of postrotary nystagmus when tested in daylight with their eyes open. As with the child having a vestibular-bilateral disorder, a short duration of nystagmus indicates that one important pathway for vestibular sensations is not being used well. Some part of the brain probably is inhibiting the vestibular nuclei too much. This does not mean that all aspects of the vestibular sensory flow are not being registered, for many autistic children with shortened duration nystagmus also show gravitational insecurity; some vestibular input is not only being registered, but because it is not modulated it is also causing distress in the child.

The autistic child's "registration" function may seem rather capricious to other people. If his brain decides to register a sensory input one day, why doesn't it register something similar on another day? This inconsistency leads a parent to say, "He could hear if he wanted to," or "Why does he like to play with one of my shoes so much, but pay no attention to one of his own?" or "If he can fry eggs for himself, why won't he set the table?" It seems as though the child is deliberately being obstinate or trying to give his parents a hard time; but this is usually not the case. The autistic child simply does not have the efficient brain that enables most of us to be consistent from one day to another or from one task to another.

The autistic child often can be motivated to register sensory input if he is given an adequate incentive. This is why behavior modification procedures are effective with these children. Sensory integrative therapy also attempts to provide an incentive for the child to register sensations, but this incentive is internal and natural. The pleasure of vestibular stimulation during therapy does help to motivate the child, and it also helps the brain to process other sensory inputs, especially visual ones. Autistic children are much more apt to look a therapist in the eye during or immediately after body movements involving a lot of vestibular stimulation.

The Modulation of Sensory Input

The autistic brain not only fails to register sensory input, but in some cases also fails to modulate input—particularly vestibular and tactile sensations. A considerable number of autistic children resist movement and are gravitationally insecure, because they cannot modulate the sensory input from the vestibular system. Sometimes they will feel comfortable swinging on a swing while in the lap of a parent, which suggests that it is not always the movement itself that causes the distress, but the lack of feeling firmly "grounded." The child seems to be extremely anxious about his relationship to gravity and space. These autistic children are greatly alarmed if someone attempts to turn them upside-down, or to put them in a high place, or to move them into an unfamiliar position. If a child is gravitationally insecure, at least he is registering some sensory input, and therapy is then more successful.

We have already noted that most autistic children do not register many tactile sensations unless those sensations are very strong. However, sometimes they not only register touch sensations, but also react to them in a defensive way.

The Integration of Sensations

Since the autistic child is unable to register many of the sensations from his environment, he cannot integrate those sensations to form a clear perception of space and his relationship to space. He may take a very long time to establish a visual percept, and even when he perceives something, he may not perceive it well. Thus an autistic child might resist wearing a new sweater, because he has not formed a familiar percept of it. He might accept the sweater more readily after he has seen it many times. It might help to wrap the sweater around his shoulders for a while before expecting him to wear it. The sensations of the sweater touching his shoulders may help him form a percept that he could not establish with visual input alone. Any new situation, such as the first few times at therapy, will present the child with a bewildering array of nonorganized sensory, and especially visual, stimuli. He is likely to react with alarm and resistance until he has repeatedly experienced that environment and can recognize it as being familiar and safe. Some children have so much trouble registering the spatial elements of their environment that they are upset whenever anything is changed in their room at home, or at therapy. Any change in the arrangement of things makes them feel insecure. Sometimes an autistic child will become upset in therapy if his mother sits in a different place than usual. We adults must have a great deal of patience and understanding to help autistic children deal with their poor sensory perceptions.

Since the recording of auditory input is inefficient, the establishment of percepts of language is limited. Likewise, without normal registration of sensory information from the skin, muscles, joints, and vestibular system, the child cannot develop a good, clear body percept. He lacks good neuronal models, both of himself and of the world, and so he cannot interact with the world. He cannot learn to plan movements well, because he cannot easily feel his body or what he is doing. He is deprived of some of the physical basis for ego development.

Wanting to Do Things

Most of us have at one time or another felt like just not moving at all. Maybe when the alarm clock went off, we were still very sleepy; or when a child called, we were lying down after a very tiring day. We knew that we should get up and take action, but something in our brains made us want to lie there and ignore the world. This feeling, which the fairly normal person experiences once in a while, is somewhat similar to what the autistic child feels most of the time.

The "I Want to Do It" Function

There is a part of the brain that is concerned with the desire to initiate behavior, to respond to sensory stimuli, to do something new or different. This part of the brain has an energizing effect; it says, "Do it!" to the parts of the brain that tell the muscles to move the body. This system works closely with the system that registers or pays attention to sensory input. The outcome of registering sensory input is the choice between doing something about those sensations or deliberately ignoring them.

Like the system that registers sensations, the "I want to do it" system is working poorly in the autistic child. It isn't that he doesn't do *anything*; rather he cannot get himself to do something purposeful or constructive. His play consists of only the most simple, repetitive actions; often merely holding onto, lining up, and whirling objects for long periods of time. More complex actions do not occur to him. If someone shows him an action, he usually does not want to do it.

The child does have some ability to play with toys or interact with the environment; and when he is given enough motivation to "turn on" the "I want to do it" system, he may be able to do some complex things, such as going through an obstacle course requiring motor planning. This system is inactive most of the time, however, and the brain rarely makes the decision to do all that it can do.

Like the system for registering sensory input, this "I want to do it" system seems rather capricious in the autistic child. A mother might try very hard to get her autistic child to do something simple like putting on a sock, while the child acts as though he will never learn, or as if he is refusing to cooperate. It may look as though the child is wilfully resisting his mother's efforts, but more likely, his brain simply cannot engage its "I want to do it" system at that time. Later he may put his sock on easily all by himself.

Part of the reason that the child does not interact with parts of the physical environment is that he does not register the meaning or potential use of many things. Knowing how to use a tricycle requires knowledge about one's body and how it works, and also some ability for abstract thinking. One must deduce from seeing the tricycle that there is a place to sit on it, that the feet go on the pedals, and that making the pedals go around will move the tricycle. Such abstract thinking is hard for the autistic child. When he sees a tricycle, and even when he registers the visual image well enough to pay attention to the tricycle, he still does not realize that it is something to sit upon and ride for pleasure. Since the "I want to do it" part of his brain is not working well, he will resist anyone who tries to get him on the tricycle.

When you present something to an autistic child, remember that he probably has the motor capacity to use it. However, his "I want to do it" system may not want to do anything new or different. If he has already learned to enjoy riding a tricycle, he may be willing to do that, but resist riding a scooter board. Before he can want to ride the scooter board, he must organize a percept of it as something familiar. To become familiar with it he needs to be on it and riding it, feeling it and his body's position and movement through his senses of touch, proprioception, and movement. Just seeing the scooter board does not give him the same understanding of it that it gives his parents or other children. Autistic children learn best through doing.

The autistic child probably does not get the normal degree of pleasure when he rides something for the first few times, since his brain may not register unfamiliar body sensations as being pleasurable. He may have to experience those sensations many times before he enjoys them. Often when autistic children are introduced to a new or different activity in therapy, they object to that activity, but after a few sessions they smile and even laugh during it. If there is to be any progress at all, both therapist and parents need to put up with the child's resistance until he is ready to accept the therapeutic activity. Most of the time the therapist cannot rely upon the inner drive of the autistic child, as she does with the learning disabled child, for the inner drive is what is malfunctioning in the autistic child.

The child's motor activity may also be influenced by poor modulation of sensations arising from gravity or movement. Gravitational insecurity will certainly give rise to unpleasant sensations unless the therapist or parent is careful in moving the child. If he cannot modulate the vestibular input, he may make himself immobile. This immobility is one of the first symptoms the therapist must deal with during therapy. Until therapy has made these vestibular sensations comfortable and pleasurable, we must expect the child to resist any effort to engage him in activities involving a lot of movement or change in body posture.

The Development of Motor Planning

Poor sensory processing hinders the development of motor planning capacity from many angles; the child cannot readily form a visual percept of the object in front of him, he does not have a well-developed body percept to use in motor planning, he has trouble abstracting the potential use of an object, he is reluctant to engage in purposeful activity, he resists doing anything new or different, and when he does do something it may not be pleasurable. For the autistic child, there is no doing for the pure joy of doing, as there is with the child whose brain is normal.

Since he does not express the innate desire to "do" and gets no pleasure from "doing," the autistic child does not develop his potential for interacting with the environment. However, some autistic children get a lot of satisfaction and pleasure out of receiving vestibular stimulation. They play on moving therapeutic equipment for long periods of time without moving on to develop more extensive interests and adaptive responses. Even when they make an effort to motor plan, they find it difficult, because they have a dyspraxic-like condition.

The most basic aspect of human behavior is the organization of percepts and the responses to these percepts. The being who cannot perceive his physical environment well, or act effectively upon that environment, lacks the basic material for organizing more complex behavior. Even though the autistic child may have normal centrally programmed movements and is not restricted by involuntary muscular contractions, he is severely handicapped in learning to use his body adaptively. He is likely to have trouble in many areas including speech, self-care, and emotionally based behavior. Since he cannot organize simple adaptive motor responses, he has trouble with all more complex behavior.

The objective of therapy for the autistic child is to improve the sensory processing so that more sensations will be more effectively "registered" and modulated, and to encourage the child to form simple adaptive responses as a means of helping him to learn to organize his behavior. When therapy does make a difference, the child's life is changed considerably; but at this time, therapy cannot make a big difference in every autistic child's life. As we continue to treat autistic children, we shall find out more about their neurologic problems and develop ways of "reaching" their brains with sensory experience.

III

WHAT CAN BE DONE
ABOUT THE PROBLEM

CHAPTER 10

SENSORY INTEGRATIVE THERAPY

As problems arise in society, so do attempts to solve these problems. As the frequency of learning disorders and brain dysfunction increases in children, more and more professionals try to figure out the nature of the problem and find a way to correct it. The first insight into the problem was that these children often had deficits in auditory and visual perception. Further study has shown that poor integration of sensations from the body and the vestibular system was the basis for some of the auditory and most of the visual problems.

Occupational therapy was originally designed to help people with motor and behavior handicaps form adaptive responses that enabled them to improve their own condition. Some occupational therapists modified these techniques to apply them to children with sensory integrative problems. These procedures have just been developed in the past 20 years, and they are still not widely known or used. Research has shown that they are effective for many, but not all, children with learning and behavior problems.

Researchers in other fields have studied how sensations from the body and interaction with the physical environment influence growth and development. This chapter first reviews some of the research on this topic, and then describes therapy in which sensory stimulation and physical interaction are used to enhance sensory integration and improve learning and behavior.

It is important to remember that our environment provides opportunities for sight, sound, smell, flavor, gravity, and some touch sensations. Our body must provide movement sensations and, through movement, the rest of our touch sensations as we move about in the world. Through movement there are muscle and joint sensations coming from inside the body. It is all of these sensations and responses to them that cause the brain to develop. Therapy involving sensory stimulation and responses to stimulation is often more effective than drugs, mental analysis, or rewards and punishments in helping the dysfunctional brain to correct itself.

Sensory integrative therapy is completely natural. Natural interactions

135

with a normal environment provide the sensory stimulation and adaptive responses that are sufficient to develop the brain in most young children. Nature designed the brain so that it would develop itself through normal physical activities. When something has interfered with this natural development *in utero* or during the first few years of life, it is best to try a natural means to remove that interference. Some children may have poor sensory integration early in life, but then largely correct the problem themselves through the natural adpative responses of infancy and childhood. If a child has a sensory integrative problem that he has not been able to correct at home and in play, he will then need special therapy to help him do what is natural.

Integration and Competence through Environmental Interaction

Until after World War II, most philosophers and scientists believed that the child's interactions with his environment had no effect on his intelligence and learning capacity. Some thought that learning capacity was predetermined before birth, so that the person could not increase his own potential. Others believed that the child was conditioned by the things that happened to him and that his own activity would not alter this conditioning.

The Swiss psychologist Jean Piaget was one of the first to recognize that the child's *interaction with his environment* was a critical factor in his development. Piaget saw that children do follow a predetermined sequence of developmental steps in which learning occurs *in response to* the things that happen. He emphasized that learning does not merely happen to us. We create our own learning process by responding to what happens.

Some specific behaviors are almost entirely the result of the way the nervous system is designed and others result from conditioning, but most of intelligence is neither predetermined nor conditioned. Intelligence is, in large part, the product of interaction with the environment. As Piaget described it, the child "accommodates" himself to his environment and "assimilates" the environment to himself. This combination of "give and take" produces an adaptive response that is effective, smooth, and satisfying. Both accommodation and assimilation develop some part of intelligence.

The child with sensory integrative dysfunction cannot adapt effectively, smoothly, and with satisfaction to a normal environment, because his brain has not developed the processes for integrating the sensations from that environment. He needs a highly specialized environment tailor-made for his nervous system. If the environment is set up appropriately, the child will be able to integrate sensations he has never been able to integrate before. Given the opportunity to do so, the brain will organize itself.

Enriched Environments and the Normal Brain

In the past 15 years, neuroscientists have shown that interaction with the environment actually improves the structure, chemistry, and function of the brain. Most of this research has been done with laboratory rats. The brain of a rat is much simpler than our brain, but the basic processes of synapse formation—as described in Chapter 3—are the same. Also, like the human brain, the brain of a rat has an inner drive to develop itself. When neuroscientists give the rat's brain more opportunity to develop, it develops more effectively.

The pioneers of this type of research have been Dr. Mark Rosenzweig and his associates at the University of California at Berkeley. However, they note that an Italian anatomist, Michele Gaetano Malacarne, did similar experiments in the eighteenth century. He found that dogs and birds who were trained for a long period developed more folds in their cerebellums than litter mates that were not trained. His findings suggest that the sensory stimulation involved in training enhanced the natural development of the brain. However, until the 1950s, scientists did not have techniques for measuring changes in the cellular structure of the brain after sensory experience.

In the experiments done by Rosenzweig and his associates, one group of rats spent time in an "enriched environment," while another group was in an "impoverished environment." The enriched environment was a cage in which there were lots of things to do, such as climbing up ladders, running in treadmills, walking over the bristles of a brush, and exploring mazes; the rats in this cage were also picked up and handled by humans. The impoverished environment was a bare cage without any of these opportunities for vestibular, tactile, and proprioceptive stimulation. After a time the rats were killed and their brains dissected and analyzed.

Rosenzweig and associates, as well as many other scientists, have done a number of variations on this experiment. In almost every case, they found that rats from the enriched environment had heavier cerebral cortices, more of the chemicals that keep the brain healthy, more of the chemicals involved in transmitting impulses across synapses, and more interconnections between their neurons. Each of these indicates that these rats had a greater capacity for processing sensations and using sensory information. Rats from the two types of environments were also tested in motor tasks. In most of these tests, the rats from the enriched environments were more successful in learning and performing a task.

A rat did not have to spend all of its time in the enriched environment to gain the benefits. Rosenzweig and his associates found that two hours a day for one month were sufficient to produce significant changes in the rat's brain. Improvements occurred in rats of every age, but were greater if the rat was very young. Similar studies with dogs and monkeys have shown the same positive results.

So scientists are now beginning to accept the idea that interaction with the environment does improve the operations of the brain. Merely seeing the enriched environment did not produce these changes; the rats had to explore that environment with their senses and their movements. The experimenters could not make the rat's brain improve; the rats had to do it themselves. That's just the way it is with therapy. The child has to organize his own brain.

There are fewer studies on the effect of environmental interaction on the normal human brain, and of course no one is going to duplicate the rat experiments with humans. The work that has been done has shown that human infants are just as responsive as animal infants. Dr. David Clark and his associates at Ohio State University have found that vestibular stimulation helped both normal children and children with neurological problems to develop better motor skills. Dr. Claudette Gregg and others at Stanford University found that gently rocking infants or letting them suck pacifiers helped their eyes to follow a moving object.

Dr. J. McVicker Hunt reviewed many studies on the effect of environments on the development of human children. He concluded that: "Intellectual competence appears to grow out of unfiltered opportunities to explore and manipulate objects and to ask questions. Effective mothers fostered development by designing a physical environment full of manipulable and visually detailed objects, things to climb on and foster motor interest, and a rich variety of things to look at."* He feels that such an environment may raise a child's intelligence quotient considerably.

Enriched Environments as a Corrective Measure

Vestibular stimulation and premature babies. The womb is an environment of frequent movement. The mother's movements rock the full-term baby for nine months. When a baby is born prematurely, he often has a hard time developing well, for he is not as well equipped to live outside the womb as he should be. A number of researchers have found that vestibular and tactile stimulation helped these premature babies to catch up with normal babies.

Dr. Mary Neal of the University of Maryland School of Nursing put a hammock in the incubator and had each premature baby rocked for half an hour three times a day. Dr. Neal found that these babies developed faster than unrocked babies in muscle tone, head movements, reaching and pulling, and auditory and visual responses. They also gained weight faster.

Others have used waterbeds to give premature infants extra vestibular stimulation, and these infants showed improved motor coordination, greater weight gain, better sucking, and more regular breathing. Why, you may ask, would rocking on a hammock or waterbed lead to such a wide range of improvements? On the surface, vestibular stimulation has little to do with body weight or breathing. However, deep inside the brain, vestibular stimulation "primes" and unifies the nervous system. For premature babies, a gain in body weight is a sign that the nervous system is doing many jobs well.

Dr. Ruth Rice had some mothers stroke, massage, and cuddle their premature infants for 15 minutes four times a day for a month after they came home from the hospital. Other mothers of premature infants did not do these things. The babies who received the extra sensory stimulation gained more weight and made better neurological and mental de-

---

*In R.N. Walsh & W.T. Greenough, Eds., *Environment as therapy for brain dysfunction* (New York: Plenum Press, 1976), p. 234.

velopment than the others did. Other studies have shown that sensory stimulation can enable premature infants to catch up with and sometimes even pass normal full-term babies.

Drs. Jerry White and Richard Labarba also found that premature babies ate more and gained more weight when given tactile and vestibular stimulation. Dr. Marlene Kramer found that extra tactile stimulation promoted premature babies' socialization with others.

Enrichment and recovery from brain damage. Experiments with animals have shown that an enriched environment helps the brain to recover from neural damage and develop healthy function. If they are to recover, the damaged neurons must be *used*; just as in normal development, development depends upon use. If the visual system is damaged, visual stimulation is necessary for the recovery of sight; if the damage is in the parts of the brain that process sound, the brain needs experiences of hearing to organize new auditory functions. However, at the same time, vestibular and tactile experiences have a beneficial effect throughout the nervous system.

Drs. Roger Walsh of Stanford University and Robert Cummins of the University of Queensland reviewed a large number of studies on therapeutic environments. They found that the critical factor in recovery was active physical interaction with the sensory environment. When the individual merely received the sensory stimulation passively, his brain did not recover. The patient must "serve as his own stimulus source." The brain must direct its own recovery by adapting to stimulation and providing itself with more stimulation. No other person can do it for him. The same is true in therapy for children with sensory integrative dysfunction.

Piaget emphasized that stimulus and response were circular. In an environment where there are many stimuli, the individual responds more often and in more different ways, and creates a greater amount and variety of stimulation for himself. During sensory integrative therapy, children often inadvertently learn specific skills or behaviors, but these specifics are not the objective. Instead we want physical activities that produce sensations that lead to adaptive responses that provide more sensations that elicit even more complex adaptive responses. In this way, the brain improves its overall efficiency of function.

The Nature of Sensory Integrative Therapy

If interaction with the environment is helpful in developing the brain, and the brain will organize itself given the opportunity to do so, then why does a child need to go to therapy? Why doesn't he give himself "therapy" at home or on the playground? The rest of this chapter will try to answer these questions.

The normal child does not have to go to therapy because play does provide him with the sensory stimulation his brain needs, and allows him to respond in a meaningful way to these stimuli. The neurologic problem in the child with minimal brain dysfunction or sensory integrative dysfunction prevents him from processing the sensations of his own play, so he cannot develop the adaptive responses that organize the brain. In other words, the child may play, but he does not play in a manner that is integrating. He needs an environment especially designed to meet his needs. Such an environment is usually not available at home or in school.

Society is placing more emphasis on language, academic, and intellectual development, and less on building the sensory-motor foundations for these higher functions. Television has captivated children so that they spend less time on swings or in sandboxes. Kindergartens are expected to teach the child to read, when they often should be providing opportunities for the child to enhance his vestibular functions—and better vestibular function would make reading easier to learn later on in school.

The sensory integration therapist is trained in the neurosciences, and can diagnose how the child's sensory systems are working and then design an environment that enables the child to interact more effectively than he has ever done before. Children with sensory integrative dysfunction often avoid following their inner drive, and so the therapist must encourage, cajole, lure, and manipulate the child into choosing the activities that will help his brain develop. She cannot organize the child's brain for him; he must do it himself, but it is evident that he cannot do it without her help.

Central Principles of Therapy

The central idea of this therapy is to provide and control sensory input, especially the input from the vestibular system, muscles and joints, and skin in such a way that the child spontaneously forms the adaptive responses that integrate those sensations. Making this idea work with a dysfunctional child requires a skilled therapist and a large room with a lot of simple yet special equipment. When the therapist is doing her job effectively and the child is organizing his nervous system, it looks as if the child is merely playing. Life is full of paradoxes; this is one of them.

Therapy is most effective when the child directs his own actions while the therapist unobtrusively directs the environment. Integration most often occurs when the child wants the stimulus and initiates an activity to get those sensations. If a child wants an activity, his brain is usually capable of organizing the sensations of that activity. The brain is designed to give itself the experiences that are necessary for its own development. This is what vertebrate brains have done for 500 million years of evolution, and this is what every child's brain is trying to do today.

The children with the more severe disorders, especially autistic children, require more external direction and structure. Sometimes fear, hostility, or other emotions will interfere with self-direction. The therapist then helps the child to release his negative emotions while he gets the sensory input he needs and makes the adaptive responses that organize that input. Hitting and kicking a cardboard box can have both sensory-motor and emotional value.

We are not trying to teach the child the activity he is doing, or any other motor skill. Teaching motor skills is the job of the physical educator. Instead our objective is to help the child function better physically, emotionally, and academically. We want to help him become more *capable of learning* any motor skill, or academic ability, or type of good behavior he needs in his life. Motor activity is valuable in that it provides the sensory input that helps to organize the learning process—just as the body movements of early animals led to the evolution of a brain that could think and read.

Diagnosis

Before we treat the child, we diagnose his problem. For children between the ages of four and nine, most therapists use the Southern California Sensory Integration Tests (SCSIT) to measure the efficiency of the child's sensory processes. These tests show how well the child is integrating vestibular, visual, tactile, and proprioceptive sensations and how well he can motor plan, make eyes and hands work together, and produce postural and eye muscle responses. She may also evaluate which systems are underreacting and which are overreacting. The therapist evaluates the child's visual perception, and sometimes auditory perception, if other professionals have not already done so. She finds out if the child has established normal hand preference and lateralization of cerebral function.

From the tests and her observations, the therapist determines where the problem is and what the child needs. Some children need primarily vestibular input; others need a great deal of tactile and proprioceptive sensations along with the vestibular input. Many need to learn to modulate the sensory input that is flooding into their brains and making them hyperactive, distractible, tactilely defensive, and/or gravitationally insecure. All children with sensory integrative dysfunction need experiences in which they produce adaptive responses, but each child needs different types of adaptive response.

Direct Application of Sensory Input

Although therapy usually involves some self-direction on the part of the child, some sensory needs can be more efficiently met by the therapist directly applying sensory stimuli to the child. Brushing or rubbing the skin sends tactile impulses flowing to many parts of the brain. Tactile stimulation can have either a facilitatory or inhibitory effect depending upon which parts of the body are brushed or rubbed, and also depending upon whether the stimulation is light or deep. The effects of touch are far more powerful than they appear to be. For this reason, untrained persons are advised not to brush the child's skin unless they are under the strict supervision of a sensory integration therapist.

Deep pressure sensations often help to organize a tactilely defensive, hyperactive, or distractible child. We often provide deep pressure sensations by putting the child between two mats to make a "hamburger." The therapist then presses down on top of the child, pretending to put ketchup, mustard, relish, and all manner of condiments on the "hamburger." Children often come out of this "hamburger" calmer and better organized than before. During other activities, the therapist may press the bones in a joint together, or sometimes pull them to stretch the joint, thereby stimulating the sensory receptors in the joints.

Vibration is an excellent way to stimulate the sense receptors in most body tissues and especially those associated with the bones. For this we use a common facial vibrator or a motor-driven vibrating board on which the child may lie, sit, or stand. Vibration of the bones sends impulses to the vestibular system. In Chapter 3, we described how the vestibular and auditory receptors evolved out of sense organs that early animals used to feel water and ground vibrations. Vibration must be used cautiously since it may affect the growing part of the bone in children.

Another form of direct sensory stimulation is through the sense of smell. Strong odors stimulate the reticular arousal system. Julia Fox found that blind children could identify objects in their hands more accurately after oil of wintergreen had been sprayed into the air. One type of sensation helps the brain process other types of sensation. One reason for this is that the reticular arousal system influences all of the sensory systems.

The vestibular sense receives the most stimulation in therapy, and this is probably what makes sensory integrative therapy effective for children who have not benefited from other kinds of therapy. It is best to let the child "serve as his own stimulus source" in choosing which piece of equipment he will use to activate his vestibular receptors. If he needs to arouse certain parts of his vestibular system, he is apt to choose equipment on which he can move rapidly and in many directions. If he needs to modulate the excess vestibular activity in his brain he may avoid all extra movement and the therapist will need to provide the proprioceptive and tactile input that helps modulate the vestibular input.

Almost invariably, the child's response to sensory input is a good guide to how well his brain is integrating the input. The therapist watches each child carefully to see the effect of the stimuli. Sometimes the effect is not immediate, but appears a half-hour or more later. Vestibular input is particularly powerful, and it can be disorganizing as well as organizing. It affects breathing and heartbeat. If the child cannot process it, vestibular input can make him unconscious or cause seizures in a seizure-prone child. Parents, teachers, and physical educators should never impose vestibular input on a child who does not want it. The use of vestibular stimuli to influence brain function should be left to the occupational or physical therapist.

Therapeutic Activity

Sensory integration occurs when a child spontaneously plans and executes a successful adaptive response to sensory input. As we described in the beginning of this chapter, the child must participate actively with the environment to improve the organization of his nervous system. The drive "to do" must come from within the child, even though he has been unable "to do" successfully before. He must take each developmental step himself, even though development has been difficult for him in the past. The equipment used in sensory integrative therapy is designed to entice the child into activities that provide sensations that tend to organize young human brains.

Sensory integrative therapy is a holistic approach; it involves the

Posed by models

Figure 3. A Scooter Board in Use with a Ramp

whole body, all of the senses, and the entire brain. When the muscles work together to form an adaptive body movement, those muscles and joints send well-organized sensations to the brain. Whole body movements also provide a lot of vestibular input, which helps to unify the other sensory systems. The ability to organize the sensations coming from the body, and to make adequate responses to them, helps the brain to organize other functions. Thus, after a course of therapy, clients say things like "It helped me pull my life together," and "I used to plan a lot of things and nothing happened; now I can pull it off."

We shall now analyze two standard pieces of equipment used in sensory integrative therapy. Both seem simple but actually they are especially designed to stimulate certain sensory systems, and to encourage specific responses to that stimulation. Responses usually reflect movement patterns of the early years of life. Those patterns build stronger foundations for the more complex reactions expected of the older child.

The scooter board. A scooter board consists of a piece of wood mounted on four wheels that can roll freely and spin in any direction. It is shown in use in Figure 3. The board is big enough to support the middle part of the child's body while his head, upper chest, and legs hang off the ends. It is covered with carpet or matting so that lying on it is comfortable.

Children usually lie in the prone position on the scooter board. They ride across the floor or down a ramp, holding both ends of the body up against the pull of gravity. Riding fast on a scooter board is somewhat of a challenge, and lots of fun.

Prone is the position in which normal infants develop many of the postural and motor responses that lead to standing, walking, and other adult sensory-motor activities. Holding both ends of the body up from the prone position at about four to six months of age is a major step in the development of sensory integration. The ability to hold this "airplane position" without a lot of effort is one of the tests for vestibular system efficiency. The forces that enable an infant to develop also operate in older children, and so we usually want the child in therapy to do a lot of things in the prone position. Fortunately most children enjoy being prone.

The prone position stimulates certain gravity receptors. As the child rides down the ramp, the acceleration activates other gravity receptors as well as the semicircular canal receptors. As the child speeds down the ramp and levels off onto the floor, the bursts of vestibular input open up pathways to many parts of his nervous system. The strong input activates reflexes that have not been developed in the past. These reflexes hold the head and legs up against the pull of gravity. The contraction of the neck muscles and the movement of the eyes as they follow what is happening send proprioceptive impulses to the brain stem, where they interact with the vestibular input. The integration of these sensory flows is very helpful to the eye muscles and makes visual perception easier.

These impulses are particularly important for organizing sensory and motor processes in the brain stem. The brain stem contributes important information about the body's relationship to space. This includes locating an object or a sound in reference to one's self, so that actions can be coordinated with that sensory information. Unless auditory and visual processes develop fairly well in the brain stem in conjuction with the processing of body and gravity sensations, they will not develop well in the cerebral hemispheres. The full body movements on the scooter board, and the sensory input and organization that go along with those movements, build a foundation for cerebral processes such as language and reading. Full body movements also provide a foundation for hand and finger movements, such as those involved in writing and using tools.

The child with adequate sensory integration rides the scooter board gracefully and without a lot of effort, because the sensations help keep his body extended. The child with an underreactive vestibular system lets his head sag and his feet drag along the floor. He must use a lot of effort to ride the scooter board and he tires quickly, just as he must use a lot of effort to learn school work and tires quickly. The child with an overreactive vestibular system may be terrified of riding down the ramp. The dyspraxic child may have trouble getting his body onto the scooter board and he may fall off easily.

The scooter board elicits sensory inputs and motor responses that cannot be obtained while sitting or standing up. As the child gradually masters these sensations and responses, his brain learns how to modulate sensory activity and forms a more accurate body percept. Fortunately riding a scooter board is lots of fun, for one ride is not going to make very much difference in a disordered nervous system. It will take many, many rides to strengthen the neural connections between the vestibular system and all the places where vestibular input is needed, and to reorganize the facilitatory and inhibitory forces that act through these connections. The therapist may entice the child to take more rides by piling up cardboard boxes a few feet in front of the ramp so that the child can ride into them and knock them down. Knocking down boxes makes the child feel strong and gives him the experience of having a strong impact on his environment. This is an experience that every child wants and needs.

When the child has mastered the challenge of going down the ramp and its novelty is starting to wear off, we give him other challenges that require more complex sensory integration and adaptive responses involving motor planning. For instance, the therapist might set up a tunnel for the child to ride through on the scooter board, or hang a ball from the ceiling for him to punch as he passes by it. Vision alone is not sufficient to guide the child in performing these tasks; the vestibular input from riding the scooter board helps him perceive the tunnel or the ball in relationship to his own body.

In the normal child, the brain puts together vestibular, proprioceptive, and tactile sensations, so that the child can *feel* how to do a task. If this integration does not happen, or if it happens too slowly, the child cannot sense where he is going or how to steer the scooter board, and so he misses the ball or bumps into the sides of the tunnel. As the child plays these scooter board games over and over again, his brain experiences sensations from each part of the body. These sensations and the resulting motor commands leave memories stored in his brain, and so the child gradually makes his body percept more accurate. The internal sensory "maps" that develop on the scooter board help the child to motor plan at home or at school. His improved sensory integration helps the parts of the nervous system that organize his thoughts and also his emotions. In addition, success in these tasks makes him feel more confident about himself.

The vestibular and proprioceptive input from riding the scooter board helps to normalize the touch system of the tactilely defensive child. This sensory input reduces hyperactivity, and also energizes the nervous system for more purposeful activity. After riding the scooter board, a child is often more calm and focused, and remains this way for some time.

It may be difficult for a parent to believe that riding a scooter board could really help his child with speech, reading, or behavior. On the surface, it seems obvious that he needs speech therapy, reading lessons, or more discipline. However, the brain is so complex that its operations are never obvious on the surface of things. If speech and reading or behavior are poor because the brain is not working well, it makes good sense to build a foundation upon which the brain can work better. After therapy has accomplished as much as it can, and if the child still has difficulty, it may be appropriate to provide him with tutoring.

The bolster swing. This piece of equipment has a strong inner core covered with foam padding and a cloth cover. It is about six feet long and three feet around. Ropes attached to each end of the bolster are

Posed by models

Figure 4. The Bolster Swing

suspended from overhead hooks.

A child can ride the bolster swing either by lying on it and holding on with his arms and legs or by straddling it. He can pull the ropes to make the bolster swing back and forth, or the therapist can swing him.

Lying down on the bolster and hanging on requires a good *flexor pattern*. Flexion is the ability to curl the arms and legs. The flexor pattern is strongly ingrained in the nervous system, and its importance can easily be seen in baby monkeys, who must flex in order to cling to their mothers. Clinging is the first full body movement that an infant makes, and so it provides many building blocks for the development of sensory-motor functions. Some children with developmental dyspraxia have not developed a good flexor pattern. Clinging to a bolster fills in some of the basic developmental steps and makes it easier for the child to develop motor planning.

The flexor pattern is especially dependent upon the integration of touch, vestibular, and proprioceptive sensations. As the child grasps the bolster, he receives a lot of touch stimulation from the covering; a lot of proprioceptive stimuli from the muscles that are contracting to hold him on the bolster; some stimuli from his joints; and a great deal of vestibular sensation from the swinging. Excitement, which acts through the limbic system and reticular activating system, helps the child to hang on tighter as the bolster swings high in the air. The therapist and child may pretend that the bolster is a bucking horse, a boat during a tidal wave, or an encounter with a whale. Some children want to develop a feeling of mastery, and they ask the therapist to swing them faster and faster so that they can find out how long they can hang on.

Riding the bolster as though it were a horse helps develop postural and equilibrium responses. If the child does not have the ability to direct himself in an activity, the therapist helps him until his brain is more organized. She sits on the bolster with the child—saying that they are "two cowboys riding to Mexico" or some other exciting place—and moves the bolster by pushing her feet against the floor, holding the child at the hips so that he does not fall off. The movement of the bolster creates a demand for equilibrium reactions, while at the same time the vestibular input makes it easier for the child to develop those reactions. The therapist carefully watches, and feels how well the child maintains his equilibrium. As his equilibrium reactions improve, she gradually loosens her hold on his hips so that he takes control. The child must learn independence gradually, and for this, he needs just the right amount of support at just the right time.

For the child who can sit fairly well, the therapist swings the bolster in every direction to activate as many of the vestibular receptors as possible. If the child needs to develop postural or equilibrium reactions, she is very careful not to swing so hard that he falls off the bolster. For this child, falling would be a nonadaptive response that would not help the brain work any better. He needs to have experiences in which his body works correctly and masters the situation. On the other hand, some children want to fall and get deep pressure sensations and emotional excitement from crashing onto the mats on the floor. If crashing is something that will help the child develop his brain, then the environment will be prepared so that he can crash without hurting himself.

The bolster swing can also be used to improve motor planning. The therapist scatters foam rubber "fish" on the mats under and around the bolster. She then swings the child, who maneuvers from one end of the bolster to the other, hanging on in any way he can, while he reaches down to pick up the "fish." The tactile, proprioceptive, and vestibular inputs help him to motor plan this "fishing trip." The fun of this activity taps the inner drive that is so necessary for neural organization.

Untrained observers see only that the child is having fun and that he is engaged in motor activity. Meanwhile the therapist sees that certain sensory systems are receiving stimulation, and certain motor responses are occurring or not occurring. She compares these responses with the child's scores on the diagnostic tests he took before therapy. She has both written reports and her own memories of how the child has progressed in past therapy sessions. As she watches the child, she relates all the information about this child to her experiences with other children with similar dysfunctions, to the published reports of therapists working throughout the world, and to research by neuroscientists. It may appear that she is merely playing with the child, but she is actually working very hard to make that "play" improve the child's nervous system. Being a therapist requires a great deal of training, imagination, and sensitivity.

Other procedures. Every child has different neurological needs, and these needs change from time to time, so therapy must provide a wide variety of opportunities for sensation and movement. For this reason, therapists have large collections of equipment for swinging, spinning, rolling, climbing, crawling, riding, and other full body movements. She also has many things that the child can pick up, manipulate, and throw. The most basic piece of equipment, though, is the child's own body.

If the child is able to do so, he chooses the equipment he will use; if not, the therapist guides him into an appropriate choice. Not all therapeutic procedures can be made entertaining. Sometimes the things that need to be done are boring or must be carefully controlled. Then the therapist will have the child do exercises that meet his needs. She must be very cautious in imposing sensory input, and she must know how to recognize when the child is becoming overloaded with sensation. Sensory overloads are not good for the nervous system, and they occur more easily and quickly in the dysfunctional nervous system. For this reason, parents and educators are advised not to impose sensory input without the careful guidance of an occupational or physical therapist.

An hour of therapy. Children with sensory integrative dysfunctions are often able to choose exactly the kind of activity that produces the sensory input and makes the motor demand that helps the child organize that input. Neuroscientists have shown that both animals and humans receive internal signals that cause them to do what is most appropriate at that moment, although the individual has no awareness of those signals. For instance, if an animal is deprived of certain vitamins, it will eat foods that contain those vitamins, even if those foods are not part of its ordinary diet. When the animal has enough of these vitamins in its body, it will return to its usual diet. Obviously the animal does not understand nutrition or have any conscious reason for its food choices, but its body tells it what to eat and how much is needed.

Children in therapy also follow internal signals. Their actions have some purpose, although the child thinks that he is just playing. Often he is putting together "building blocks" for some future development. Here is what one learning disabled child with shortened duration nystagmus chose to do during an hour of therapy. I could not have chosen better for him, and had I tried to do so, he would probably have done the activities with less enthusiasm and therefore accomplished less. We shall call this child "Bill."

First Bill chose to play "net hockey" with his therapist. Each lay prone in a net that hung from an overhead hook. They were about 10 feet apart and close enough to the floor to push themselves about with their hands. With plastic "hockey sticks" they hit a soft ball back and forth, usually keeping it on the floor and sometimes bouncing it off the walls. To reach the ball, they had to swing themselves sometimes in one direction, sometimes in another, sometimes back and forth, and sometimes in an arc. All this movement generated an enormous variety of vestibular input. Because of his underreactive vestibular responses, Bill's head grew heavy and his neck tired, but the excitement of the game kept him at it. The strong contractions of his neck muscles to hold his head up against gravity generated a lot of proprioceptive input, and so did the movements of his eyes in following the ball. Both the vestibular and proprioceptive sensations helped Bill aim his stick at the ball. His brain stem and cerebral hemispheres worked together to integrate the vestibular, proprioceptive, and visual stimuli.

Next Bill chose to ride with another client in the "helicopter," so named because two children sit upright in separate seats and spin around like the blades of a helicopter. The centrifugal force from spinning in an orbit stimulated Bill's gravity receptors in a way different from that of lying in the prone position in a net. Holding the head and body upright against this force required strong contractions of the flexor muscles in the front of the neck and body opposite to the contractions needed to hold the body up from the prone position. So Bill's internal directions guided him to choose two activities—net hockey and then the helicopter—that stimulated different vestibular and muscle receptors and therefore complemented each other to achieve a well-rounded effect.

The helicopter offers very intense vestibular stimulation, and Bill apparently needed a lot of this input, for he rode it for about 10 minutes. Then he chose to use the Play Buoy. This is a plastic buoy that can move freely along two ropes about 15 feet long. Bill held one pair of ends while his therapist held the other. Each of them had to throw hands and arms out in a coordinated manner to send the buoy along the ropes to the other. Meanwhile their eyes had to shift focus from near to far and back to near. Like many children with shortened duration nystagmus, Bill had trouble using the two sides of his body and his eyes in a well-coordinated manner. However, after having "primed" his brain with so much vestibular input on the helicopter, he was able to process the sensations and movements of the Play Buoy more effectively than he could have otherwise.

Next Bill rode on the "whale," which is a seat held up by an elastic rope. The child sits on the seat with his legs touching the mat and bounces himself up and down as if he were riding on the spout of a whale. This provided Bill with vestibular stimulation in the vertical plane. This vertical movement further complemented the horizontal stimulation of net hockey and the rotary stimulation of the helicopter. Meanwhile, Bill looked at and spoke to his therapist. This created a demand for efficient eye stabilizing, since Bill's eyes had to remain focused on a stationary target while his body went about four feet up and down.

By this time, Bill had apparently given his brain as much vestibular stimulation as it could organize. He chose to build a structure by placing mats over a small jungle gym. This activity involved exploring visual space, and all of that vestibular and proprioceptive input had certainly prepared his brain to organize visual perception. During this time, Bill hid from his therapist and then jumped out with a "Boo!" Hide and go seek is a common stage that children go through, both in normal development and in therapy, when their improved vestibular functions allow them to relate more effectively to space. Hiding gives the child a feeling of mastery over both space and other people. Children enter this hide-and-go-seek stage on their own without encouragement or demonstration from others. They sometimes strain the patience of people who do not realize the full significance of this game for the child's growing sense of identity. Indeed, it isn't too impressive as a therapeutic activity, but it does give the child what he needs.

Bill's academic performance improved rapidly during the time he was in therapy. He began to show progress after just a couple of months, which is more quickly than in children whose emotions interfere with their pursuit of sensory integration. Bill improved rapidly because he had a strong inner drive to seek the stimuli he needed, and was able to follow his own internal directions.

The Therapeutic Atmosphere

One of the objectives of therapy is to strengthen the child's inner direction so that he will be better able to direct himself in life. Most education is externally directed, and probably needs to be that way most of the time. But children also need to develop inner direction in their relationships with the physical environment and other people. Self-confidence is based on the ability to direct oneself.

The locus of personal control begins to form in the second and third years of life when the child begins to realize that he and his mother are separate beings and that he has some mastery over himself. As we saw in Chapter 2, mastery at that age consists of walking, climbing a little, building things, and changing things in the physical and social environment. The child can run away from his mother and say "no" to her. The more integrated the child's nervous system, the better he will be able to establish this independence.

Most children with sensory integrative problems have very little self-confidence. It is hard to feel all right about yourself when that self is not all right. Furthermore, the dysfunction makes them less competent than others. As young children they discovered that they couldn't do what their friends did, and they compared themselves unfavorably. They began to feel inferior and impotent, controlled by external forces, and bound to failure. Many juvenile delinquents have grown up feeling this way.

Children sometimes come to therapy afraid to do anything but the most elementary activities. They are afraid to do things that are well within their capabilities. They don't want to show how poor they are at doing things. They have learned that other people usually expect too much of them or find fault, and so they are afraid that their therapist will do the same. All of these fears make the child resist his own inner drive and avoid activities that would develop his sensory-motor functions. When this happens, the therapist must spend time dealing with that resistance. She must help the child learn to trust her and the therapeutic environment.

Since only the child can organize his own brain, the therapist must tap his inner drive by offering the child challenges at which he is likely to succeed. The activities available in the therapeutic room must all be geared to the child's sensory integrative needs and capacity. They must be enticing rather than threatening to a child who is easily threatened. The therapist is there to help the child give himself vestibular, proprioceptive, and tactile experiences, and make adaptive responses that are more advanced than those the child has already accomplished.

If the environment is optimal for this child's growth, he will feel that therapy is "fun" and be eager to come to therapy. As he begins to realize his latent potential, and experience self-fulfillment with his better-organized nervous system, he shows a greater zest for therapeutic activities. His enthusiasm tells the therapist that the environment is giving the brain what it needs to develop.

The child with a well-organized nervous system shows that zest during most of his free play. It is fun to encounter the challenges of gravity, movement, and motor planning. Adults experience that same exhilaration when they express their inner drive for sensations and movement. Some need very intense vestibular and proprioceptive stimuli to feel this joy, so they climb mountains, parachute jump, or drag race. For others, the milder sensations of dancing, swimming, or jogging are sufficient.

The inner drive toward sensory integration exists in most young children, but often lies buried under a sense of inadequacy and failure. It takes a great deal of skill and imagination to provide a playful, nonthreatening environment in which the child can direct his own growth. It takes courage to let the child appear to waste time as he fumbles and resists and explores his own way. If he cannot explore by himself, the therapist intervenes, assists, and cajoles the child to bring out what the child cannot quite bring out by himself.

The therapist tries carefully to balance structure and freedom in a way that leads to constructive exploration. This balance is not easily achieved. Free play does not inevitably, in itself, further sensory integration. If it did, many children with dysfunction would have solved their own problems. But too much structure does not allow growth either. With this balance of structure and freedom, the therapist helps the child develop both his neural organization and his inner direction. The child is given as much control over therapy as he can handle, as long as his activity is therapeutic. The therapist controls the environment, while the child controls his own actions. Self-confidence, or an improved attitude about one's self, is often the first change parents notice in their children after they have started therapy. The child is more in command of his life because his nervous system functions better.

Comparison of Sensory Integrative
Therapy with Other Approaches

Sensory integrative therapy is a specialty of occupational therapy, a profession that has emphasized understanding human behavior from a neurobiological viewpoint. The term "occupational" means that the therapist helps the patient or client to perform some purposeful activity. Most activities in sensory integration therapy are purposeful, since the child has a goal in doing them. Doing purposeful physical activities—rather than thinking or talking about them—is the best way to improve human functioning when the problem lies in the way the brain is working.

Psychotherapy. Sensory integrative therapy is different from classical psychotherapy in that it attempts to help the child cope with life's demands by helping the brain to be more efficient. Psychotherapy usually is concerned with analyzing the relationships among people and talking about why people do the things they do. Lying on a psychotherapist's couch is not a good way to develop a brain that needs sensory stimulation and adaptive body responses, but it might be a good way later on to understand one's situation from an intellectual point of view.

The two forms of therapy do have some things in common. In both cases the client must do the work himself, while the therapist is there to help make the work possible. In both therapies, there are times when the client "spins his wheels" and doesn't seem to be making much progress. Since the only way to grow is through one's own effort, growth is bound to have both rapid and slow periods. That's the best anyone can do.

Play therapy. There is a form of psychotherapy for children known as "play therapy." Since sensory integrative therapy looks like play, one might think that it is a type of play therapy, but it isn't. Play therapists do not think in terms of the effect their work is having on the child's brain, and they are not trained to promote sensory integration. Play therapy is a psychodynamic approach; the therapist is trying to get the child to have certain emotional and social experiences. Sensory integration therapy is, of course, concerned with emotional and social growth, but only as end products of more basic sensory integrative functions.

Perceptual-motor training. Sensory integrative therapy is not perceptual-motor training, which is teaching the child specific perceptions and skills such as doing puzzles or playing hopscotch. Specific motor skills are good to learn for their own sake, but do not expect them to help a child academically. Teachers and physical educators may provide training in perceptual-motor abilities, but they are not trained to assist the child in improving the way his brain works.

Education. Schoolteachers are trained to approach the child intellectually without concern for whether the child has the neurological foundation for intellectual functioning. Therefore most educational tasks are appropriate for those children with normal sensory integration, but many tasks are too advanced for children with minimal brain dysfunction.

Education is concerned with *what* the child learns; sensory integrative therapy with *how* he learns or *why* he doesn't learn. The therapist is trying to develop the whole child for learning anything within his intellectual capacity.

Why Does Sensory Integration Therapy Work?

The research discussed in the beginning of this chapter helps to answer this question. A few more comments specific to children with brain dysfunctions are in order. Brains—especially young brains—are flexible and capable of natural change. As the brain matures, some of this flexibility is lost. If the child is young enough to grow new connections among his neurons (under two years) then therapy might help him do so. If the child is older, therapy appears to facilitate the transmission of messages from one neuron to another so that these messages flow with greater ease and efficiency. If there is too much inhibition in the brain, the sensory input overrides these inhibitory processes. If the child is overly responsive, the input and adaptive responses help to modulate the activity in the neural connections that are already there.

Sensory integrative therapy works because the brain is designed so that the functions that are used are the functions that are most likely to develop. It works because the therapeutic environment is set up so it is fun for the child to use his sensory processes in a way that he could never use them before. It works because almost every human being has an inner drive toward sensory integration, and therapy is simply a way to do what nature, the child, and his mother were not able to do.

There are some children who will not be helped by sensory integrative therapy, even though their problem is a learning disorder or sensory processing problem. Sometimes the problem is severe and we do not have the knowledge required to treat that severe a problem. Sometimes we cannot determine the nature of the problem with enough clarity to design an effective program for that child. Sometimes the problem is in a part of the brain that is less dependent upon the organization of sensations from the body, and these children profit more from special education.

A Case Study

Bob—a fictitious name for a very real boy—was eight years and 11 months old when he was first tested for sensory integration. (A therapist prefers to see a child at a much earlier age, since the younger brain has a better chance of changing.) Bob was in his fourth year of school, but his reading ability was that of a first grader. His spelling and math were the same as a child who had completed most of the second grade. Because he scored almost as well as most other children his age on intelligence tests, Bob was placed in a special class for learning disabled children.

Diagnosis

Bob was tested on sensory integration, language skill, and academic achievement. His postrotary nystagmus was of short duration. He had trouble standing on one foot with his eyes closed, although his postural and equilibrium reactions were generally adequate, but not especially good. He could manage most playground activities without feeling bad about himself, although in the tests he had a hard time motor planning. He had no trouble knowing which finger was touched when he could not see his hands, and he had a good sense of where his hands were in space without looking at them. But he did have trouble discriminating touch stimuli, and sometimes could not tell the difference between a square and a triangle in his hand. His perception of visual space and form was also poor for his age. In addition, he was hyperactive, distractible, and tactilely defensive.

Bob's scores on auditory and language tests were also below those expected of a child of his age and intelligence. He had considerable difficulty understanding what was said to him, especially when there were other noises at the same time. Another test showed that both sides of his brain tended to process language sounds equally well. His hands had nearly equal motor abilities, but neither hand was especially good.

From these tests and clinical observations, we determined that Bob's basic sensory integrative deficit was in his vestibular system. This vestibular processing problem caused him to have a learning problem and difficulties in motor planning, eye-hand coordination, visual perception, and language development. The vestibular sensations that his brain could not process contributed to his being hyperactive, distractible, and tactilely defensive.

Therapy

Fortunately Bob showed a great desire for vestibular stimulation, since that is what he most needed. He spent many hours swinging on a swing having a single elastic rope, and so he went up and down, as well as around and back and forth. If I had not learned to trust children's inner drive and direction, I would not have let him spend so much time doing the same thing over and over. Sometimes I did feel that maybe I should be arranging a more varied kind of program; but I allowed his inner drive to direct him.

In time, Bob did choose something else. After four or five months in therapy, he started to climb—anything and everything available—and then jump down from wherever he had climbed. Apparently Bob had given himself enough vestibular input on the swing to open up pathways to many parts of his brain. Climbing enabled him to use those new pathways and relate to more of his physical environment. He almost had a few accidents, because his new-found desire to explore his sensory-motor potential exceeded his ability for motor planning. The pathways opened by the vestibular input also enabled Bob to learn to read more easily. Before therapy was completed, Bob was placed in a regular classroom full time.

As often happens when a young boy's nervous system becomes better organized, Bob developed a need to demonstrate his new-found abilities by having a greater impact on the physical world. He would hold on to a rope hanging from the ceiling and swing himself around, kicking a cardboard barrel that went careening around the room with a lot of noise. The experience of making a large object move so rapidly gave the appearance that this boy was "macho," and this is part of what Bob needed to experience. Because he was in therapy, Bob was able to do this in a way that allowed him to pass through this stage. It would have been impossible in a home or classroom. At the same time, Bob developed a great willingness to help keep the clinic orderly, as if he wanted his therapy room to be as well organized as his brain was now becoming.

Results of Therapy

A year after the first testing, Bob was given some of the tests again. During the year, he had received about six months of therapy, two and one-half hours a week. He showed definite gains on both language and visual perception tests. The duration of his postrotary nystagmus had not changed. (This finding was *not* interpreted to mean the vestibular system had not improved. Natural and normal inhibitory factors act on nystagmus as a result of a lot of vestibular stimulation.) His reading was now appropriate for a child finishing the fourth grade—a gain of more than three years in just one year. His spelling was that of a child who had been in the fourth grade for two months—a gain of one and one-half years. His arithmetic was at the level of a child entering the third grade—a gain of less than one year. So therapy seems to have significantly improved Bob's ability to learn academics, especially reading.

REFERENCES

Chee, Francis K.W., Kruetzberg, Jeffrey R., & Clark, David L. Semicircular canal stimulation in cerebral palsied children. *Physical Therapy*, 1978, *58*, 1071-1075.

Clark, David L., Kreutzberg, Jeffrey R., & Chee, Francis K.W. Vestibular stimulation influence on motor development in infants. *Science*, June 10, 1977, *196*(4295), 1228-1229.

Fox, Julia V.D. Improving tactile discrimination of the blind. *American Journal of Occupational Therapy*, 1965, *19*, 5-11.

Gregg, Claudette L., Haffner, M. Ellen, & Korner, Anneliese F. The relative efficacy of vestibular-proprioceptive stimulation and the upright position in enhancing visual pursuits in neonates. *Child Development*, 1976, *47*, 309-314.

Hunt, J. McVicker. Environmental programming to foster competence and prevent mental retardation in infancy. In R.N. Walsh & W.T. Greenough (Eds.), *Environment as therapy for brain dysfunction*. New York: Plenum Press, 1976.

Kantner, Robert M., Clark, David L., Allen, Lynn C., & Chase, Marian F. Effects of vestibular stimulation on nystagmus response and motor performance in the developmentally delayed infant. *Physical Therapy*, 1976, *56*, 414-421.

Korner, Anneliese F., Kraemer, Helena C., Haffner, M. Ellen, & Cosper, Lorna M. Effects of waterbed flotation on premature infants: A pilot study. *Pediatrics*, 1975, *56*, 361-367.

Kramer, Marlene, Chamorro, Ilta, Green, Dora, & Knudtson, Frances. Extra tactile stimulation of the premature infant. *Nursing Research*, 1975, *24*, 324-334.

Montgomery, Patricia, & Richter, Eileen. Effect of sensory integrative therapy on the neuromotor development of retarded children. *Physical Therapy*, 1977, *57*, 799-806.

Neal, Mary. Vestibular stimulation and developmental behavior of the small premature infant. *Nursing Research Report*, 1968, *3*, 1-5.

Rice, Ruth Dianne. Neurophysiological development in premature infants following stimulation. *Developmental Psychology*, 1977, *13*, 69-76.

Rosenzweig, Mark R. Effects of environment on brain and behavior in animals. In E. Schopler & R.J. Reichler (Eds.), *Psychopathology and Child Development*. New York: Plenum Press, 1976.

Solkoff, Norman, & Matuszak, Diane. Tactile stimulation and behavioral development among low-birthweight infants. *Child Psychiatry and Human Development*, 1975, *6*, 33-37.

Walsh, Roger N., & Cummins, Robert A. Neural responses to therapeutic environments. In R.N. Walsh & W.T. Greenough (Eds.), *Environment as therapy for brain dysfunctions*. New York: Plenum Press, 1976.

White, Jerry L., & Labarba, Richard C. The effects of tactile and kinesthetic stimulation on neonatal development in the premature infant. *Developmental Psychobiology*, 1976, *9*, 569-577.

CHAPTER 11

WHAT PARENTS CAN DO

The importance of parenting is vastly underestimated. More than anyone else, parents can make a world of difference in helping the child with a learning or behavior problem develop better sensory integration. Without parents who understand and support his development, the child will have a lot of difficulty and probably be unhappy; he may drop out of school. With the understanding and support of their parents, most of these children do lead worthwhile and satisfying lives.

The principles and ideas in this chapter can be used with any child. In most children there is still room for development in brain functions. Some children with severe neurological problems can be helped only a little by parents or therapists, but this chapter can help parents manage such children and care for their needs.

There are five important things that parents can do: (1) recognize the problem so that you will know what your child needs, (2) help your child to feel all right about himself, (3) control his environment, (4) help him learn how to play, and (5) seek professional help.

Recognizing the Problem

Mothers are usually correct; if things aren't just right with her child, a mother will usually know it. She usually can't quite put her finger on what's wrong or convince her pediatrician that there is a problem. She may even tell herself that everything is okay, but still wonder why her child has so many problems in life. If she has had other children, she may realize that this child is not developing as the others did. She may notice that he is more fussy and cranky, can't tolerate many things, and is not easily comforted.

A mild problem in sensory integration is particularly hard to recognize. The child often seems completely normal—except for his unusual difficulties with school work—and so no one suspects that there is disorder in the way his brain functions. If your child seems bright enough, but does not respond well to the demands of kindergarten or first grade, you should immediately consider the possibility that he has a sensory integrative dysfunction.

Children do develop at different rates, but one of the biggest mistakes a parent can make is to think that the child will outgrow his problem. If therapy is to be effective, the brain must be young and flexible. Do not wait until he is older and less able to benefit from therapy.

Another mistake is to think that an educational or intellectual approach alone will help the child—as though he could be trained to do things his brain is not able to do. When a learning disabled child is placed in school too early, or in a school that makes many demands upon children, he will compare himself unfavorably with the other children and develop the feeling that he is inferior. The best place for a child with a mild neurologic dysfunction is a noncompetitive nursery school with teachers who promote sensory-motor development, but also understand and allow for different rates of development. It may help to delay sending the child to kindergarten until he is one year older than his classmates and better able to cope with school.

Catching the problem early in life will not always prevent the problem from occurring, but it will at least give the child a better chance of reducing the effects of that problem on his life. Early recognition will certainly help the family see the child's behavior in the proper perspective so that they can give him the extra acceptance, consideration, and structure he needs. If your child is behind in development, do not immediately jump to the conclusion that he will have problems; instead, do something to help him develop his sensory integrative processes. It is important to remember not to push the child into doing things he is not ready to do; rather, give him the opportunity and encouragement to do things his brain can handle.

One of the common errors made by professionals today is to assume that behavior problems can be corrected without doing something to change the brain dysfunction producing those behaviors. The psychotherapist tries to change the relationships in the family; the school counselor wants the child to think differently and form new decisions; the behavioral psychologist tries to condition the child to certain behaviors. Each of these approaches is appropriate at certain times, but they often fail because the child's poor sensory integration causes the problem to recur. It is not enough merely to change family dynamics, or mental processes, or specific behaviors. The sensory integrative therapist helps the child to organize his nervous system and then these things change naturally.

No one lives without stress and demands. Nothing goes perfectly for anyone. A brain that is not well integrated is going to have a lot of trouble with life. The child with minimal brain dysfunction is apt to relate poorly to people unless they make allowances for the irregularities in his nervous system. The problem may seem "psychological," but the psyche is regulated by the brain. Before you spend a lot of time and money on psychotherapy to change interpersonal relationships, it is better to try to help the brain work better first. Then, if there still are problems, psychotherapy may help.

It is easy to recognize unpleasant behavior, but more difficult to recognize the nervous system organization that underlies that behavior. When a child behaves poorly, it is important to realize that a great deal of that poor behavior may come from ordinary sensations that this child cannot integrate. If he cannot organize sensations, he cannot organize his behavior. This is why learning and behavior problems occur even in children who have good family relationships.

A delay in speech development is another clue to sensory integrative dysfuction. Speech depends upon many sensory-motor functions, and so it is often delayed whenever any part of the brain does not work efficiently. The ability to form words is particularly related to the vestibular system as well as the auditory system.

The major objective of this book has been to help parents recognize sensory integrative problems for themselves. One cannot expect physicians to do so, because they are not trained along those lines. When a pediatrician says that there is nothing wrong with your child, interpret that to mean there is nothing wrong in the areas he has evaluated. And then look for yourself; if a sensory integrative dysfunction is there, you will see some of the signs. Learn to use professionals wisely. A doctor can do something for medical problems; but do not rely upon him solely for your child's well-being. An educator can teach the normal child school subjects; but do not expect him to enhance your child's capacity for learning.

Help the Child to Feel All Right About Himself

A neurological disorder is handicap enough, but on top of that disorder the child usually has the additional handicap of a negative self-image. There are three things that contribute to that negative self-image: the way in which the nervous system is functioning, the feelings of frustration and inadequacy that arise when the child cannot do things well, and other people's negative reactions to what the child does. Parents can do a great deal to counteract the negative reactions of other people, and they can do quite a bit to reduce the feelings of frustration and inadequacy.

A Physical Problem

The first step is to realize that the child's problem is a *physical* one. It involves the action of electrical impulses and chemicals in his brain. A learning disorder or behavior problem resulting from brain dysfunction is just as much a physical problem as a broken leg or the measles.

When a person has the measles, he does not feel up to par; he is apt to be irritable and may be cranky and less likeable. More things go wrong, because the physical problem of the measles interferes with the way the person behaves. We forgive and make allowances for the person with the measles. Similar forgiveness and allowances must be made for the child with a sensory integrative problem. You may not approve of the child's behavior, but do not let your disapproval damage the child's concept of himself as a person. Let him know that people don't like it when he behaves poorly, but that this does not mean no one will ever like him. Also help him to know what things are socially acceptable and then help him to do those things.

If a child is sick and vomits on the living room carpet, you can say, "Next time try to make it to the bathroom," but don't punish him or make him feel ashamed for not making it there. Similarly, don't punish a child or make him feel ashamed because his coordination is poor, or because he can't learn to read or write, or because he can't control his bowels, or because he does things that make other children dislike him. This is the child who needs parental love and acceptance more than the child who doesn't have such problems. This is the child who needs a world of emotional support to help him become likeable.

It is extremely hard to be accepting when a child is disruptive, stubborn, uncooperative, mean, or hostile. It tries the patience of even the most tolerant parent. It takes more patience than any parent should be expected to have. How does one cope with this type of behavior? If you remember that the child has a physical—though not visible—problem, you may find it easier to accept his behavior and disposition. You can still love him and he can love you back. Your child's feelings about himself will in part reflect your feelings about him.

Foreseeing Emotional Crises

Recognize that his nervous system is not as stable as other children's. This makes him emotionally fragile. Too much stimulation—movement, people, confusion, changes in schedule, noise, demands, illness—can cause him to lose control of his emotions. This is especially true if the child is tactilely defensive or gravitationally insecure. Learn to sense when your child is about to lose control of himself. For instance, birthday parties are the most stressful of activities for some children. When you sense that your child will not be able to cope with certain stimuli, remove him from that environment or decrease the amount of stimulation from the environment. Children do not like to lose control, because they feel worse about themselves when they do. You can help your child preserve a good self-concept by steering him away from situations that may overwhelm his nervous system. You can also help him by being calm yourself; you are a major part of your child's environment, and your emotional state will affect his nervous system.

Instead of Punishment

If your child does lose his temper or self-control, punishment will only lower his self-concept even further. The child feels bad enough about losing control; punishment will make him also feel guilty and embarrassed. Instead of punishment, the child needs something that will help him regain his composure. A quiet place, such as his own room, away from the stress will help more than anything else. When the brain becomes disorganized, don't think punishment. Instead, think of controlling the sensory input from the environment to help organize that brain.

First reduce the sensory overload, and second, provide sensations that are organizing. A furry toy, a favorite blanket, or a familiar pillow provide the type of sensations the child needs. Hugging or holding the child is even better for some children. Rocking in a rocking chair may help. For the younger child, a tepid bath may be soothing. Slow rubbing *down* the middle of the back increases the organization of the brain; do not rub up the back, for this moves the hairs on the skin opposite to their direction of growth and may produce defensive reactions. Outdoor activities will provide proprioceptive input that may calm the child's nervous system—especially if the weather is cool, since cool air helps to modulate the impulse flow from the skin and often reduces hyperactivity.

Discipline

This does not mean that you should not discipline your child. Every child needs discipline at some times. Rewarding good behavior and taking away privileges (such as watching television) for inappropriate behavior is a basic principle of discipline. Don't get into a debate with your child over discipline; simply tell him what you are doing and why you are doing it. Once you make a decision that your child can or can't do something, stick with it. So think twice before you say "no." To be effective, discipline must help to organize the child's brain, rather than disorganize it. Therefore you must be consistent, aware of what you are doing, and sensitive to the effect you are having on your child's nervous system.

Expectations

Parents sometimes damage their child's self-concept by having expectations that are too high for him to fulfill. Because we cannot see a sensory integrative dysfunction, it is easy to forget that the child has a handicap and cannot do as well as other children. Make sure that your expectations for your child are within the capacities of his particular nervous system.

If a person is blind we do not expect him to see, nor do we criticize him for not seeing. However, if a child can see, we expect him to avoid bumping into things. Unfortunately, although the child with a disorder in space and form perception can see, he cannot get the proper information from what he sees. Therefore he sees a chair, but bumps into it anyway. Since he doesn't *always* bump into things, and can avoid them by paying very close attention, people think that he deserves criticism when he does bump. A more considerate approach would be to remind the child that he needs to look very carefully at where he is going. If he does bump into something, a casual "oops" may be enough. He hardly needs to be told that he shouldn't bump into things; he already knows that. "It's hard to avoid bumping, isn't it?" would tell the child that you know what he is experiencing and are "on his side." The same understanding and support is needed when the dyspraxic child breaks his toys ("Yes, sometimes it's hard to know how to play with things"); when the gravitationally insecure child refuses to play with other children ("You want to play that game, but it's kind of scary"); or the tactilely defensive child gets mad at you when you are touching him ("I know that this doesn't feel very good").

Accentuating the Positive

You can promote your child's self-concept by noticing and commenting upon the positive things that he does. This reinforces the good behavior and increases the likelihood that the child will repeat that behavior. Even if it's just a little thing, your child may feel a lot better if you praise him for it. Accentuating the positive and ignoring the negative is a good general rule. Even the child with a severe behavior problem does some good things. Make a point of telling him that you approve of these things. This will help him realize that he can behave well.

The child with a sensory integrative problem who is accepted and supported by his parents is the one who can make a go of it in life. Another child with a similar problem of the same severity, whose parents do not recognize the problem and who criticize the child because of the symptoms, is the one who will, at best, struggle through life, and, at worst, become a juvenile delinquent.

Control the Environment

The type of home life parents provide is extremely important in any child's development. The sensations of home life bombard the child's brain for much of each day, while therapy can provide only a few hours of sensory input a week. Therapy will obviously be most effective if the child spends the rest of his day in a well-organized environment.

Structure

Structure in the environment often helps the unstable brain preserve its stability. Good organization of one's life and home will promote good organization of the brain. Organization centers on *time* and *place*. Each activity has its own time and each moment has its own activity. Each object has its own place, and most of the time, the object is in that place. Teaching the older child how to organize time and objects is one of the best things a parent can do to help the child compensate for a poorly organized brain. Good organization is a form of self-discipline, and the child with a sensory integrative problem will have to learn self-discipline, for it usually does not come naturally.

The Tactile Environment

The parts of the environment that touch the child's skin can have the greatest effect, negative or positive, on his nervous system. Respect your child's response to sensory stimuli. Remember that not everyone experiences sensory input the same way. What may be a comfortable touch to you may be completely uncomfortable for your child. Being touched by you may be all right, while someone else's touch may cause a defensive reaction. Clothing that feels soft to you may feel itchy to your child. For one child a furry stuffed animal may provide just the right tactile experience, while for another child it may be distasteful. To one child, a little extra rubbing on the arms and face after washing may be calming, while to another it may make no difference.

A dark tunnel made of cloth tubing or blankets is a dandy thing to crawl into to cut down on overly stimulating environmental input; be sure that air can get through the cloth for breathing. Or the child can roll up in a soft old bedspread to get touch and pressure sensations that calm his nervous system. The comfort that comes from a "security blanket" is caused by the touch stimulation from many parts of the body, and this furthers the integration of the nervous system. Young children have not developed any of the cultural "shoulds" or "should nots" about touch, and so their physical responses are a good guide to which tactile input is good for their nervous systems and which is not. Just watch and listen to your child.

Negative reactions are a clue that the child needs some extra tactile input that is acceptable. Sleeping between beach towels or in terry cloth pajamas may provide the tactile impulses that balance the activity within the nervous system. Or perhaps it will help to sleep with an extra pillow wrapped in a towel and lying beside him. Before the child goes to bed give him a light back rub. After the bath, give him extra drying with a towel. But watch his reaction closely; if he doesn't like the input, respect his wishes.

Remind your relatives that the child's rejection of their hugs and kisses is not a personal matter; it may be a matter of his nervous system not being able to feel those sensations comfortably. The reaction would be the same no matter how the child feels about the person touching him. If your child automatically hits someone who accidentally touched him, explain that it was an automatic reaction that the child could not control. It would also be appropriate for the child to apologize.

Vestibular and Proprioceptive Experiences

Children's responses to vestibular input may be just as varied as their responses to tactile input. Some love it; some do not. To impose vestibular stimuli on a child who cannot modulate them can damage his emotional development, and certainly will not help his nervous system develop. Adults often think that tossing a child into the air or holding him upside-down is a friendly act; and after reading this book, they may think that it is therapeutic. However, for the child with gravitational insecurity, such an experience may cause intense distress.

Merely rocking in a rocking chair may be as much as a particular child can tolerate. Some children feel all right when they rock with the head in one position, but not in another position. Some children are reluctant to lie on their stomachs and may have to sleep on their backs. Especially watch your child as he plays; any irregular response to vestibular input is a cue to seek professional help from a sensory integration therapist.

If your child seeks a lot of vestibular stimulation, give him an environment in which he can move his body. Running, jumping, or climbing outdoors, or playing on equipment that lets his body move a lot, will help settle his nervous system. Household chores in which he has to lift, carry, or push things may provide welcome proprioceptive stimulation. Remember that physical work does more than simply build muscles; it provides sensory input and adaptive responses that organize the nervous system.

We have said that the child's relationship to gravity is even more important than his relationsip to his parents. That statement does not mean that parents are not important. Part of the job of a parent is to help the child develop his relationship to gravity. You introduce your child to gravity by picking him up, carrying him, and rocking him, and by putting him in a cradle, stroller, or baby swing. As he grows older, you can extend that relationship with backyard swings, pony rides, swimming, hikes in the hills, and trips to the beach. The child who dislikes these activities, or who gets tired easily, is often the child who needs them most. Never force your child into these activities, since he is the one who must organize his brain. Make them available and simplify them so that he can handle them. If he can't, then let him choose his own way of stimulating his brain.

Auditory and Olfactory Sensations

Some children are overly sensitive to sounds or smells that occur in the home. Sounds that the child cannot modulate can be very irritating and interfere with the child's attention. The yells and screams of other children may be extremely annoying. Some children suffer when fire engines go by. If your child seems uncomfortable, listen for the cause of that discomfort. It may help to close the windows or to take the child into another room. Also try to modulate your own voice so that it does not over-arouse him. Speaking in a whisper may calm down his nervous system.

Odors that do not offend adults or other children may be quite offensive to the child who is hypersensitive to the sensations from his nose. Such odors may come from food, household chemicals, the toilet, automobile exhaust, and many other sources. Your child may dislike certain people because of subtle body odors that only he notices.

The most important thing for a parent to do is to realize that the child simply perceives things differently. To some extent, he can be protected from overwhelming sensations, but parents cannot deal with every sound and odor in the environment.

The Warning Signs

Your child will give you warning signs if you or something in the environment is making too many demands on him. He is most apt to become hyperactive or distracted. He may become hostile and aggressive, or withdrawn and weepy. Other people may consider him stubborn. His behavior may simply deteriorate. Sometimes the observant parent will see these warning signs and change the situation before it gets any worse. At other times, her intuition will warn her to change the situation before the signs appear.

Helping Your Child Learn How to Play

Society tends to underrate the importance of play. Since most children play adequately without parental help, and since it is not easy to see how play develops the brain, most people think of play as mere entertainment or "fooling around." However, the child's play before he goes to school is just as important for his development as his school work. Some mothers know how to help a normal child play, but most have difficulty helping a child with a neurological handicap.

If a child does not play with as many different things as other children, parents tend to think that he is just not interested in that type of play. However, the child who is not interested in normal play probably has a problem, and that problem usually includes a sensory processing disorder. The dyspraxic child's play is very limited because he has trouble motor planning and so he must stick to simple and familiar games. The child with a vestibular problem is restricted by his poor postural responses or by the anxiety caused by vestibular input that he cannot modulate. The tactilely defensive child may avoid playing with other children because he does not like their touching him. Some children with poor sensory processing are embarrassed when other children see their clumsiness, and some simply cannot organize their behavior well enough to play productively.

The essential ingredient in play is the child's expression of his inner drive toward self-fulfillment as a sensory-motor being. The end product of play—for example, a tower of blocks or some number of jumps over a jump rope—is not important in itself. What is important is that the child follows his inner drive to produce physical activity in which he masters his environment and his body. Physical activity produces sensory stimulation and adaptive responses that help to organize the brain. The external results may not mean anything to an adult, but to the child they signify success in his own growth process.

Through play the child obtains the sensory input from his body and from gravity that is essential for both motor and emotional development. The sensory input is what makes it "fun." Running, turning, bending, touching things, pushing, pulling, rolling, crawling, climbing, jumping, and so on produce a tremendous amount of vestibular, proprioceptive, and tactile input. One of the reasons children play is to get this input. They need lots of it while they are young, and less as adults. The more the child explores, the more his senses are stimulated and the more complex the adaptive response required. The more varied his play, the more it contributes to his development.

Play is essential for developing the capacity to motor plan. As he plays, the child moves his body parts in countless different ways, and the sensations from these movements add new sensory "maps" to his body percept. Through large full-body movements, he learns how to relate himself to the space around him. Through manipulation of small playthings, he learns to use his hands and fingers efficiently. Play expands competence. The child may not need this competence until later in life, but he won't develop much competence unless he plays effectively as a child.

Watch your child closely when he is playing and try to recognize the significance of what he is doing. When he is joyful, that joy may come from some sensory-motor experience that his brain needed very much. Be happy with him. Show him that you want him to encounter challenges in which he can master his body and his environment. It's all right if he gets dirty or bruises himself, for those things are inevitable as he pushes himself to make more and more mature responses.

On the other hand, if he becomes overexcited or sad or hostile during play, realize that these feelings may come from some failure in sensory-motor processing. It may not be something that you notice, but still be a major setback for the child.

Such experiences can stop a child from learning, or they can be steps on the way to mastery. If you give him a lot of emotional support without trying to control what he does, he will probably try the task again and again until he masters it. Above all, your child wants you to show some concern for his problem; not the kind of concern that says, "This is what you should do; now do it," but the kind of concern that says, "I know that you can learn how to do that, and I will do whatever I can to help you learn whenever you are ready."

Remember that play is primarily directed by the child's inner drive. If you push him into playing, some of the benefits will be lost. Instead, set up an appropriate situation and show the child how to do each thing until he can do it himself. Don't tell him intellectually; show him physically. Make favorable comments to help him feel that he can succeed; accentuate the positive and ingore the negative. Fantasy and imagination will keep him interested in trying again and again; a pile of sand can be "the great desert," and digging holes can be "looking for treasure." Use your imagination, and your child will gain more from his play.

Try not to make him feel more inadequate by expecting him to do things he cannot do. This will defeat the purpose of play. Parents tend to provide playthings and activities that are too complicated for the child with sensory integrative dysfunction. If the child balks at some type of play, it may very well be beyond his sensory-motor capacity. Try something more elementary. True, it's harder to think of the simpler things.

If you were playing catch with a normal child, you could expect him to catch the ball with more, or at least the same, skill as you continued playing. The normal child learns from practice and retains what he learns, because he can keep his nervous system organized. However, do not have the same expectations when you play catch with a dysfunctional child. The irregularities in his sensory-motor processes will make his performance irregular. He may improve for a few minutes or days, and then lose it. Be patient and let him stumble about, and reach for the ball at the wrong time, and throw it way off to your side. This is what he needs to do in order to learn, and he will learn more easily if you are patient. Also help him to learn how to do it better. Even if he does not make any spectacular catches or throws, but enjoys what he is doing, he is probably putting together the "building blocks" in his brain. Your job is to back him up at every step along the way.

Children do not need expensive toys to play effectively. Often a child will prefer to play with an old spoon, or a bedsheet, or some other household item. In fact, spoons and bedsheets may help your child develop greater sensory integration than he would with an expensive toy. Playthings should give the child lots of opportunities to use his imagination and creativity, and the child should not have to worry about breaking the object as he explores it.

Empty cardboard cartons and plastic bottles, tires or inner tubes, large ropes, kitchen pots and pans, pieces of foam padding, pillows, and other things lying around the house offer valuable opportunities for play. Don't worry about what the child will do with them; he will think of something.

Sandpiles are great; cut up a bleach bottle or plastic soap container for use as a scoop. Water and sand are a good combination. Dirt can be shoveled; holes can be dug in it; mountains made in it or tunnels dug through it; toy cars can be driven over it. Digging sand or dirt provides a lot of proprioceptive and tactile input. It's worth the mess for mother.

A simple bolster can be made of an old blanket or two tied into a roll. The child will have fun simply rolling over it. Try making an obstacle course in which the child must creep, crawl, climb, step up, walk backwards, hop, and jump. Change the obstacles every time he goes through it successfully so that he has to produce new adaptive responses. Roughhousing provides a lot of touch and muscle and joint sensations from the strong contractions of the muscles.

The games that children have played for centuries are especially good ways to develop sensory integration. Hide and go seek is a good way to develop space perception and a body percept, since the child must look for a place large enough to hide his body. Hopscotch develops equilibrium responses and motor planning. Bean bag toss involves eye-hand coordination.

When you buy toys, choose ones that will encourage your child to move his entire body or manipulate things with his hands. Tricycles, wagons, jumpropes, slides, swings, rocking horses, jungle gyms, blocks, puzzles, Tinker Toys, Lego, etc. are all good. Toys that are merely pushed or pulled around—like a toy dog on wheels—do not offer much in the way of sensory stimmulation or demand for adaptive responses. The best toys have no set use, but offer many variations in use so that the child must use his imagination to create his own play.

Backyard playsets offer basic sensory-motor experiences, and playground equipment provides even greater vestibular and proprioceptive inputs. When you take your child to the playground, remember that his responses to swinging, spinning, sliding, and so on may be underreactive, overreactive, or irregular. Help him to express his inner drive on the equipment. Also watch out for other children who might try to play too roughly with a child who cannot protect himself.

In addition to watching for your child's response to stimulation, it is also important to watch out for his safety. Always assume that a child with a sensory integrative problem will be accident-prone, although some children compensate for this by being overly cautious. Your child with sensory deficits will need more protection than other children, since he does not process all the sensory information he needs for his own protection. Watch out for objects on which he can cut or bruise himself or things into which he can run or fall; either keep him away from these dangers, or keep them away from him, or help him to pay attention so that he doesn't hurt himself. Assume that he is going to have an accident, ask yourself where and how, and then take preventive measures.

Bumps and bruises are inevitable and all right if they occur along with experiences of mastery. Don't worry about them unless they interrupt your child's play. Children who are tactilely defensive often overreact to minor skin injuries. If your child's bumps and bruises make him cry, then you should hug or rock him, or give him emotional support in some other way, and then let him go back to playing. Show your child that cuts and scrapes are not major catastrophes. Help him to realize that his body is resilient and will heal itself. A sense of trust and security within one's own body is basic to well-organized brain functions.

Seek Professional Help

If you think that your child has a sensory integrative problem, take him to a qualified occupational or physical therapist with special training in sensory integration procedures to either verify or discount your suspicions. Of course, have the child checked out by a physician to see if there are medical problems. However, do not expect your doctor to know about or look for sensory integrative disorders, learning problems, or even minimal brain dysfunction. These areas are not covered in a standard medical school education. Some physicians who have specialized in pediatric neurology will be able to detect the problem and help your child.

.To find a sensory integrative therapist who can test your child and advise you about therapy, call the nearest hospital that specializes in children and ask for the Occupational Therapy Department. If there is no children's hospital, try a large general hospital. Remember that sensory integration therapy is practiced only by occupational therapists or physical therapists who have been trained in sensory integration.

Do not delay in seeking help. If the child has a sensory integrative problem, he will probably not outgrow it. He may learn some way to cover up and compensate for the problem, and make it so subtle that you do not notice it; but the disorder will still be inside his brain making his life difficult.

If your child begins to show academic problems in kindergarten or first grade, do not wait until he decides that he is a failure or until the school tells you that he has a learning problem. Once a child begins to think that he cannot learn, he begins to block himself emotionally. His negative thoughts and feelings about himself will make learning even harder, and perhaps give him a personality problem.

The longer you wait to give him treatment, the slower the treatment will work, and so he will need more treatment and it will help him less. The younger the brain, the more flexible and easy to influence it is. Everything that can be done in early childhood to help the brain develop more efficiently will give the child more ability to cope with learning and emotional demands later in life.

Do not expect a schoolteacher, physical educator, or movement educator to give your child therapy. They are trained to teach skills to children, not to help the dysfunctional brain develop. Let them do their own jobs. If you think that your child has a sensory integrative problem, tell his teachers what to expect. A teacher can do her job better if she knows that one of her students has a special problem that he cannot help. If your child has a learning problem, his teacher may be able to work with him on his own level so that he can learn more.

Parents carry the responsibility of coordinating their child's health and education programs. They must see that medical treatments, school, exercise programs, and therapy work together. The more they know about each program, the more they can fit everything together, and the more they can carry out at home. Sensory integration is a new idea among professionals, although the natural inclination of children has always been to follow its principles. New ideas are not readily accepted in long-established fields of practice. The medical professions are especially conservative and will often reject a new idea until it has been established for several generations. Your child can't wait that long.

This book has been written to help you, the parent, make judgments on your own—to help you be responsible for seeing that your child receives the best opportunities for development.

SOME QUESTIONS PARENTS ASK—
AND THE ANSWERS

Do all poorly coordinated children have learning problems—or vice versa?

No, on both counts. Poor motor coordination can be caused by many different things, some of them having very little to do with sensory integration. It is true that poor sensory integration *often* results in poor coordination or clumsiness. However, we see many children with sensory integrative problems who have adequate coordination. Children with either poor coordination or learning problems should be checked out by a sensory integrative therapist to see if therapy will help them.

Do learning disabled children really see backwards?

I don't think so. I suspect that some of the time they can't remember, even for a moment, the spatial orientation in a simple scene or picture. Since they don't store accurate visual images, they get "b" and "d" mixed up. Maybe they see "b" as "b," but think of it as "d."

What's the difference between perceptual-motor training and sensory integrative therapy?

In perceptual-motor training, the child is taught specific perceptual memories or motor skills—for instance, that a triangle is going one way or another, or how to find hidden figures within complex designs, or how to hop, skip, jump, or walk on a narrow board. It is fine to learn these things, but doing so does not necessarily help the brain to work more efficiently in other tasks. In contrast, the sensory integration therapist's objective is to make the child's brain work better, and he *may or may not* learn new percepts or skills.

This doesn't look like therapy. All you're doing is playing with him!

The children here or in any treatment situation do many things that give their brains lots of vestibular, tactile, and proprioceptive stimulation. This stimulation is one of the things that normal play provides the average child. However, the child with sensory integrative dysfunction rarely gives himself the proper stimulation at home. If this child had been able to develop normally all by himself, without help, then he wouldn't need to be treated here. He has to come to therapy to have someone guide him in doing the things that will help his particular nervous system work better.

Therapists are aware of the sensory and motor functions that are poorly developed in the children who are here. They are trying to help the child engage in an activity that will fulfill his needs and allow him to form an adaptive response that will develop the functions in which he is having a hard time. If we didn't make it seem like play, a child would not participate with the enthusiasm that is necessary for effective therapy. No one can organize a child's brain for him. He has to do it himself, but he can do it himself only if he is doing what he calls "play." It takes a tremendous amount of skill to make this therapy look casual. It may look like play to you, but actually both therapist and child are working very hard. All of the activities here are purposeful; they are all directed toward a goal. And the goal here is self-development or self-organization.

What is self-organization?

A child is self-organized when he can play at one thing in a constructive manner for a reasonable length of time. He is not self-organized if he starts doing one thing and then almost immediately goes to something else. He is not self-organized if his play is nonconstructive—if he just throws blocks around rather than building with them. He is not self-organized if his teacher has to remind him to sit at his desk and do a specified task already requested of him. Children learn to organize themselves through play, provided the nervous system is able to do so.

Can't my child get the same things from playing in the backyard at home? We have a backyard set with swings and a slide and a sandbox.

Splendid. Encourage their use, but there is a lot of difference between what your child will do at home in his backyard and what he will do here in therapy. At home, he will do the things he can do on his own, and they will benefit him somewhat. In most children, play in the house and backyard is enough. However, in children with sensory integrative dysfunction, disorganization in the brain interferes with the processing of play sensations and also with the child's knowledge of how to play. If a child has grown up with a problem in development, then he probably needs to do something different. The therapist will help him to do the proper things. She is trained to help children with sensory integrative problems do the things that will organize their nervous systems. The play at home will certainly help that organization. By all means, continue the swinging and climbing in the backyard.

Is his brain damaged?

In a few cases, it may be damaged, but we can't tell which ones these are. All we can say is that, judging from the results we get on diagnostic tests, the child's brain is not functioning the way it should. We use the word "dysfunction" rather than damage; the word means that his brain is not functioning well. When the stomach is not working well, we call it "indigestion" rather than stomach damage. Most of the irregularities of function that occur in the brain are not caused by damage.

Some experiments have shown that when there is actual damage in a child's brain we probably bring about less change through therapy than when there is only dysfunction. In either case, we never make things perfectly all right, we just make things better.

Was there something wrong in the way we raised him?

Sensory integrative problems usually do not stem from the way a child is raised. They are more often the result of conditions we do not understand very well. Poor nutrition, chemicals in our food or air, problems at birth, and many other factors may cause problems in certain children; but since we cannot see inside anyone's brain, we cannot trace the problem back to its cause. It would be hard to escape modern civilization, but sensory integration therapy is a natural, drugless way of treating these problems when they do arise in children today.

Don't many of these children grow out of the problem by themselves?

If a child has a sensory integrative problem, he will not "grow out of it." With a lot of practice and effort, he may learn "splinter skills" (see Chapter 4) that compensate for poor sensory processing and cover up the problem. A child with disorganized postural and eye muscle responses may learn to play baseball and write with a pencil, but he has to do so in spite of his neurological disorder. Learning splinter skills is the hard way to do it, and it leaves the child with less energy for other things. In therapy, we are trying to make things work more easily for the child, and this can happen only when his brain works in a more integrated way.

If he tries real hard, can't he succeed? He's a bright, hard-working child.
Will power is not a very efficient way to make up for what the nervous system isn't able to do easily. Certainly your child may be able to spend all of his energy in school work, maintaining his balance, moving his eyes, or thinking about how to move; but then he will have a lot less energy for other things like paying attention to what's being said. Will power should not be necessary for these functions.

Of course, will power does come from the nervous system, but it doesn't come from the parts of the nervous system that integrate sensation. It's better to develop the parts of the brain that make sensory processing easy, rather than trying to do it with will power. Sensory integration makes many things easier, although they may never be easy; but will power can be used only for a few things at any one time.

Working hard may help, but it is not the way to overcome the problem, and brightness is also not enough. A child may work very hard and with a lot of intelligence, but because he is working and thinking with a poorly organized nervous system, he will still have troubles. The sensory integrative approach is to help the brain work more efficiently, so that the "work" is easier.

You say that a child should be allowed to follow his own inner drive. Does that mean letting him run about whenever he wants?
The drive to do things—to move and play constructively—is essential to normal growth and development. Children with neurological dysfunction may have the drive to do things, but their poor brain organization prevents their being constructive, so their inner drive does not serve them well. Almost all children have an inner drive to organize and develop their vestibular systems. Every child likes to run and tries to climb. If he climbs and falls, or runs and trips over his feet, he may lack sensory-motor competence. If your child hurts himself when he follows his inner drive, then you need to construct his environment in such a way that he can follow his inner drive without hurting himself.

Running about at random is not the same as following the inner drive. Random activity is not organizing. Many children with disorganized brains need to have strong structures around them. You put a child who is not well organized into a wide-open space, and he will run all over that space because he cannot organize himself in space. This may give him a lot of vestibular and proprioceptive input, but it will not help him to organize those sensations.

Do children get hurt often in therapy?

No, not seriously, but they often get little bumps and bruises. We are constantly aware that our clients are accident-prone, but for optimal development they must also be allowed to engage in activities in which injury is a possibility. Because we recognize that ever-present possibility of being hurt, we take as many precautions as possible. There are mats wherever a child might fall more than a few inches. Equipment is covered with carpet. Therapists work on a one-to-one basis. Only a few therapists in this field have reported serious injury. Those who are not properly trained or who do not really understand the dysfunctioning child are less likely to provide the same protection as the trained therapist.

Should I bring my child to therapy even when he is having a bad day?

Yes, unless he is ill or has had an accident. A therapeutic situation is the best place to handle temper tantrums or whatever happened that made your child have a "bad day." Remember that when we treat brain dysfunction, we are treating the psyche or personality just as much as the rest of him. If he is upset or negative, his nervous system is probably working even less efficiently than usual. Maybe therapy will help smooth things out.

What should I tell him about going to therapy?

If he is old enough to understand, tell him that he is coming "to play," and that this may help him to read or speak more easily, or enjoy life a little bit more, or whatever. If he is old enough, he may be able to understand some of what has been said in this book. If he is younger, he probably won't ask after the first time, and will be satisfied with the answer that he is coming "to play." You want the child to come with enthusiasm, since he has to put a lot of himself into therapy to benefit from it. But he will want to come to therapy not because of what you tell him, but because of how it makes him feel.

What should I tell him to help him get along in school and with other children?

The most important thing you can do for your child is to let him know that he is loved and accepted just the way he is. When there is love and acceptance at home, the child will be more apt to develop a feeling of confidence in himself. Self-confidence will help him more than anything to relate to peers and handle life in general.

Last week he came running home crying because no one would pick him for a baseball team. What would you have said to him?

I'd say, "Yes. That's rough, isn't it?" Don't deny the problem. Just recognize that he's feeling bad, as matter of factly as possible, and then try to find something that he can do successfully.

What kinds of toys should we get him?

Big things: slides, swings, teeter-totters, tricycles, wagons, play cars, jungle gyms; and the kind of things we use in the clinic: scooter boards, inner tubes, large mats and cushions. Tinker-Toy-type sets are good for indoor play. The poorest toys are things that the child just pulls around or that run around on batteries. There is not much to be gained from playing with toys that cannot be manipulated. Toys should promote imagination. The simpler a plaything is, the more opportunities it offers for many types of play. Many of the best toys can be made out of household items or inexpensive materials.

My child watches television for five hours a day. What should we do?

There are some good children's programs, but if he spends that much time watching television, he is not getting the amount of sensory input he needs from play. Play is a very important aspect of development, and I'm talking about interacting with large playthings, moving his entire body, and responding to a lot of vestibular, proprioceptive, and tactile sensations. A child with sensory integrative dysfunction needs more of that play than a child who has been more fortunate, and he also needs special guidance in that play.

Can his teacher in nursery school or kindergarten help him get the right sensory input?

Nursery and kindergarten teachers can certainly help development a great deal, but they aren't trained in the neurosciences. They have other important tasks such as helping children learn to relate to each other. They can't be expected to be therapists. Until recently, all nursery schools were places where children played, and so they were already doing a good job. I would like to see every nursery school and kindergarten emphasize sensory-motor activities and language development instead of setting the child down at a desk and teaching him to read or compute. With learning disabilities on the increase, it would be appropriate for kindergartens to assume a strong role in laying the sensory-motor foundations for academic achievement. The increased emphasis on early reading is all right for those who have the neural organization to cope with it. However, many children don't have this degree of integration at age five, so they experience early failure and a loss of self-confidence.

What do you think of special education programs?

Special education programs are essential. Even with the enhanced neurological efficiency that comes from sensory integration therapy, most children still need academic help. Furthermore, some children have problems that can't be helped very much through therapy. In those cases, special education offers the most help. However, it doesn't make much sense to give a child something to read when he is deficient in sensory processing, which *can* be *developed*. That's like trying to make a poorly baked cake taste good by putting more icing on it. Special education tries to teach the child in spite of his problem, instead of doing something about the problem itself.

If special education were completely successful, these children wouldn't be here getting therapy. Sensory integrative therapy has been developed to approach the child in a much more normal, natural way. It attempts to *prepare* the child to learn. It helps many children to learn more easily, but it does not help all of them.

Why didn't our doctor say something about these problems?

The average physician does not know how to look for these types of dysfunction, and so he doesn't see them. Physicians are trained to look for diseases or other conditions that are more severe and more obvious. Every child who is having trouble should be checked by a physician for medical problems. Physicians are the appropriate source for medications, but do not rely on them to see the subtle nuances of behavior that indicate a sensory integrative problem. We hope that in the future medical schools will place enough emphasis on minimal brain dysfunction to enable pediatricians to recognize the importance of the problem and tell parents when the child can profit from sensory integrative therapy.

What about the educational psychologist at school?

Educational psychologists are trained to recognize learning disorders, but they usually don't have a background in the neurosciences. They see that the child is having trouble with academics or with behavior, and they know how to make appropriate changes in the school program, but they cannot be expected to understand the brain dysfunctions that are at the core of these problems. Do not expect them to treat sensory integrative dysfunction.

Can psychotherapy help my child?

A child whose brain isn't working very efficiently is bound to have trouble with his family and other people. Life is full of stresses and one cannot avoid them. The psychotherapist sees that the child is having a hard time coping with life, and he tries to explain interpersonal relations to the child and his parents so that they can cope better. Both sensory integrative therapy and psychotherapy deal with the same problems, but psychotherapy tries to deal with the problems by talking about them, while sensory integration therapy aims to help the brain work better. Sensory integration is far more basic than rational or cognitive processes. I suggest that you first see what we can do to help your child's brain work a little bit better. When we have done as much as we can along that line, if there are still problems, then let a psychotherapist talk to your child. However, if you are very uncomfortable, have your child do both forms of therapy at the same time.

Are there drugs that can improve learning or behavior?

Some physicians do use drugs to help the brain calm down, but sensory integration therapists do not use these drugs. Other people suggest that one be concerned for nutrition, for what we eat and drink has a profound influence on the brain. However, these topics are outside my field, and so I can't make any recommendations about them.

Should we massage or brush our child at home?

If the therapist recommends it, there are some things that you can do to provide extra tactile stimulation. It is best to first let a therapist test the child before trying to do anything yourself. Of course, you can hug and touch your child, and this will contribute to the development of his tactile system; but do not deliberately try to do therapy on him. It is enough to be a loving and affectionate parent.

Is there anything that pregnant women can do?

I recommend that pregnant women rock in a rocking chair for five or 10 minutes twice a day. The vestibular system begins to form and mature about the tenth week in utero, and so the vestibular system is operating throughout the last six months before birth. At any time in life, rocking is a pleasant way to influence the vestibular system. During pregnancy, it might be a good preventive measure. Some therapists have rocked during a pregnancy and found that this child had better postural development than their other children.

GLOSSARY

The following is a list of words used in this book and their definitions. The numbers in parentheses refer to chapters in which these terms are explained in detail.

Adaptive response: An appropriate action in which the individual responds successfully to some environmental demand. Adaptive responses require good sensory integration, and they also further the sensory integrative process. (1, 2)

Aphasia: The inability to speak and, sometimes, difficulty in understanding the spoken or written word. (5, 6)

Apraxia: The lack of praxis or motor planning. When seen in children, a sensory integrative dysfunction that interferes with planning and executing an unfamiliar task. (6)

Auditory: Pertaining to the sense of hearing. (3)

Autism: A form of brain disorder affecting the child's ability to relate to people, things, and events. (9)

Body percept: A person's perception of his own body. It consists of sensory pictures or "maps" of the body stored in the brain. May also be called body scheme, body image, or neuronal model of the body. (3, 6)

Brain stem: The lowest and innermost portion of the brain. The brain stem contains nuclei that regulate internal organic functions, arousal of the nervous system as a whole, and elementary sensory-motor processing. (3, 4)

Central programming: The neural functions that are innate within our central nervous system; they do not have to be learned. Creeping on hands and knees and walking are good examples of centrally programmed actions. (6)

Cerebellum: The part of the brain that is wrapped around the back of the brain stem. It processes proprioceptive and vestibular sensations to help make body movements accurate. It also processes all other types of sensation. (3)

Cerebral cortex: The outer layer of the cerebral hemispheres. It includes areas for very precise sensory processing, especially of visual and auditory details and sensations from the body. It also executes fine, voluntary body movements and speech. It is concerned with thoughts, mental evaluations, and goals. (3, 4)

Cerebral hemispheres: The two large sections of the brain that lie over and around the brain stem. The hemispheres continue the sensory processing that begins at lower levels and assist in producing voluntary motor responses and behavior.

Cocontraction: The simultaneous contraction of all the muscles around a joint to stabilize it.

Cranial nerves: The set of nerves running from the head and face directly to the brain (without passing through the spinal cord) and from the brain back to the head and face.

Dyspraxia: Poor praxis or motor planning. A less severe, but more common dysfunction than apraxia. (6)

Extension: The action of straightening the neck, back, arms, or legs.

Facilitation: A neural process that promotes the conduction of impulses or a response to them. Facilitation is the opposite of inhibition. (3)

Flexion: The act of bending or pulling in a part of the body.

Gravitational insecurity: An abnormal anxiety and distress caused by inadequate modulation or inhibition of sensations that arise when the gravity receptors of the vestibular system are stimulated by head position or movement. (5)

Inhibition: A neural process that reduces the conductivity of certain synapses so that some impulses are blocked. Inhibition performs an important function by reducing excess neural activity. Unlike in other fields of psychology, the neurologic term "inhibition" does not have a negative connotation. (3)

Labyrinth: From the Greek word for "maze." The complex bony structure of the inner ear. It contains both the vestibular and auditory receptors. (3, 5)

Lateralization: The tendency for certain processes to be handled more efficiently on one side of the brain than on the other. In most people, the right hemisphere becomes more efficient in processing spatial and musical patterns, while the left hemisphere specializes in verbal and logical processes. (3, 4)

Learning: A change in neural function as a consequence of experience. (1, 2, 3, 10)

Learning disorder: A difficulty in learning to read, write, compute, or do schoolwork that *cannot* be attributed to impaired sight or hearing, or to mental retardation. (1, 4)

Limbic system: The parts of the cerebral hemispheres concerned with emotionally based behavior and emotional response to sensory input. The limbic system receives and processes input from all sensory channels. (3)

Locomotion: Movement of the body from one place to another.

Modulation: The brain's regulation of its own activity. Modulation involves facilitating some neural messages to produce more of a perception or response, and inhibiting other messages to reduce excess or extraneous activity. (3, 4)

Motor: Pertaining to body movement or posture.

Motor planning: The ability of the brain to conceive of, organize, and carry out a sequence of unfamiliar actions. Also known as praxis. (6)

Neuron: The structural and functional unit of the nervous system. It consists of a cell body with terminals for receiving nerve impulses and a fiber capable of sending impulses.

Nuclei: A cluster of nerve cell bodies that organize and integrate sensory and motor activity. In a way, they are "business centers" for the operations of the brain.

Nystagmus: A series of automatic, back-and-forth eye movements. Different conditions produce this reflex. A common way of producing them is by an abrupt stop following a series of rotations of the body. The duration and regularity of postrotary nystagmus are some of the indicators of vestibular system efficiency. (5)

Occupational therapy: A profession that employs a purposeful activity to help the client form adaptive responses that enable the nervous system to work more efficiently. (10)

Percept or perception: The meaning the brain gives to sensory input. Sensations are objective; perception is subjective. (3)

Postural background movements: The subtle, spontaneous body adjustments that make overt movements of the hands, such as reaching for a distant object, easier. These postural adjustments depend upon good integration of vestibular and proprioceptive inputs. (5)

Praxis: See *Motor planning*.

Prone: The body position with the face and stomach downward.

Proprioception: From the Latin word for "one's own." The sensations from the muscles and joints. Proprioceptive input tells the brain when and how the muscles are contracting or stretching, and when and how the joints are bending, extending, or being pulled or compressed. This information enables the brain to know where each part of the body is and how it is moving. (3, 6)

Protective extension: The reflex that extends the arms to provide protection when the body is falling.

Receptor: A cell or group of cells that are sensitive to some type of sensory energy. Receptors transform the sensation into electrical impulses and send them over sensory nerves to the spinal cord or brain. (1, 3)

Reflex: An innate and automatic response to sensory input. We have reflexes to withdraw from pain, startle at sensations that surprise us, and extend our head and body upward in response to vestibular input. There are many other reflexes, (2, 3)

Reticular core: The central core of the brain stem, and one of the most complex and entangled portions of the brain. Every sensory system sends impulses to the reticular core, which then sends influences to all of the rest of the brain. (3)

Sensory input: The streams of electrical impulses flowing from the sense receptors in the body to the spinal cord and brain.

Sensory integration: The organization of sensory input for use. The "use" may be a perception of the body or the world, or an adaptive response, or a learning process, or the development of some neural function. Through sensory integration, the many parts of the nervous system work together so that a person can interact with the environment effectively and experience appropriate satisfaction.

Sensory integrative dysfunction: An irregularity or disorder in brain function that makes it difficult to integrate sensory input. Sensory integrative dysfunctions are the basis for many, but not all, learning disorders. (4)

Sensory integrative therapy: Treatment involving sensory stimulation and adaptive responses to it according to the child's neurologic needs. Therapy usually involves full body movements that provide vestibular, proprioceptive, and tactile stimulation. It usually does not involve activities at a desk, speech training, reading lessons, or training in specific perceptual or motor skills. The goal of therapy is to improve the way the brain processes and organizes sensations. (10)

Southern California Sensory Integration Tests (SCSIT): A series of tests designed to assess the status of sensory integration or its dysfunction.

Specialization: In general, the process by which one part of the brain becomes more efficient at particular functions. Most specialized functions are lateralized, that is, one side of the brain is more proficient in the function than the other side.

Synapse: The place where two neurons make electrochemical contact and also the transmission of a nerve impulse from one neuron to the next. Neural impulses travel a path of many synapses, and each synapse adds to the processing of those impulses. (3)

Tactile: Pertaining to the sense of touch on the skin. (3, 7)

Tactile defensiveness: A sensory integrative dysfunction in which tactile sensations cause excessive emotional reactions, hyperactivity, or other behavior problems. (7)

Tonic neck reflex: The reflex that makes an arm tend to extend when the head is turned toward that arm. The other arm tends to flex at the same time. It should be integrated into the overall function of the brain the first few months of life, but remains overly active in many children with brain dysfunctions. (5)

Tract: A long, thin bundle of nerve fibers that carry sensory input or motor responses from one place in the nervous system to another. (3)

Vestibular-bilateral disorder: A sensory integrative dysfunction caused by underreactive vestibular responses. It is characterized by shortened duration nystagmus, poor integration of the two sides of the body and brain, and difficulty in learning to read or compute. (5)

Vestibular nerve: The fibers of the eighth cranial nerve that carry vestibular input from the gravity receptors and semicircular canals to the vestibular nuclei. (3, 5)

Vestibular nuclei: The groups of cells in the brain stem that process vestibular sensory input and send it on to other brain locations for organization of a response. These complex "business centers" also integrate vestibular input with input from other sensory channels. (3, 5)

Vestibular receptors: The sense organs that detect the pull of gravity and the movements of the head. They are located in the labyrinth of the inner ear. Each inner ear contains gravity receptors in tiny sacs and movement receptors in semicircular canals. (3, 5)

Vestibular-spinal tract: The pathways for neural messages from vestibular nuclei to the motor neurons in the spinal cord. Vestibular-spinal messages help to maintain muscle tone, hold the body upright, and keep the joints extended. (3, 5)

Vestibular system: The sensory system that responds to the position of the head in relation to gravity and accelerated or decelerated movement. (1, 2, 3, 5)

Visual: Pertaining to the sense of sight.

INDEX